## Books by James Wright

### Poetry
*The Green Wall* (1957)
*Saint Judas* (1959)
*The Branch Will Not Break* (1963)
*Shall We Gather at the River* (1968)
*Collected Poems* (1971)
*Two Citizens* (1973)
*Moments of the Italian Summer* (1976)
*To a Blossoming Pear Tree* (1977)
*The Summers of James and Annie Wright* (1981)
*This Journey* (1982)
*The Shape of Light* (1986)
*Above the River: The Complete Poems* (1990)
*Selected Poems* (2005)

### Prose
*Collected Prose* (1983)
*In Defense Against This Exile: Letters to Wayne Burns* (1985)
*A Secret Field: Selections from the Final Journals of James Wright* (1985)
*The Delicacy and Strength of Lace* (with Leslie Marmon Silko) (1986)
*A Wild Perfection: The Selected Letters of James Wright* (2005)

### Translations
*Twenty Poems of Georg Trakl* (with Robert Bly) (1961)
*Twenty Poems of César Vallejo* (with John Knoepfle and Robert Bly) (1962)
*The Rider on the White Horse and Selected Stories by Theodor Storm* (1964)
*Twenty Poems of Pablo Neruda* (with Robert Bly) (1967)
*Poems by Hermann Hesse* (1970)
*Neruda and Vallejo: Selected Poems* (with Robert Bly and John Knoepfle) (1971)
*Wandering: Notes and Sketches by Hermann Hesse* (with Franz Wright) (1972)

# Selected Poems

# JAMES WRIGHT

# Selected Poems

Edited by Robert Bly and Anne Wright

Farrar, Straus and Giroux / New York

Wesleyan University Press / Middletown, Connecticut

Farrar, Straus and Giroux

Printed in the United States of America
Published by Farrar, Straus and Giroux and Wesleyan University Press
First edition, 2005

Library of Congress Cataloging-in-Publication Data
Wright, James Arlington, 1927–
    [Poems. Selections]
    Selected poems / James Wright ; edited by Robert Bly and Anne Wright—
1st ed.
        p.   cm
    ISBN-13: 978-0-374-52902-4
    ISBN-10: 0-374-52902-7 (pbk. : alk. paper)
    I. Bly, Robert.   II. Wright, Anne (Edith Anne).   III. Title.

PS3573.R5358A6 2004
811'.54—dc22
                                                                2004041167
Designed by Jonathan D. Lippincott

www.fsgbooks.com

10   9   8   7   6   5   4   3   2

Frontispiece photograph by Katharine D. Saltonstall

Picture on page xiii by Nicholas Crome

To Galway

# Contents

# Preface
by Anne Wright

I thought for a long time about making a selection of James's poems. While *Above the River*, which contains the complete poems, is to me a beautiful book, it is, perhaps, too heavy or a bit overwhelming for a new reader. A substantial selection would be easier to carry about, slip into a suitcase, or read in bed. It would also serve as an introduction to James's poetry and whet the reader's appetite for more.

The poet Robert Bly, our very close friend, also had a selected poems of James's in mind. We discussed working on this project together several years ago and decided to be coeditors.

Since I am not a poet and had never worked on a selected before, I had no idea how difficult this undertaking would be. As I went through James's work, book by book, I gained a thorough understanding of how each volume was tightly woven, how the exquisitely careful order of the poems formed an almost unbreakable pattern. No wonder James always quoted Robert Frost as saying that if you have a book of twenty-four poems, the book itself should be the twenty-fifth.

If a selected poems was going to happen, the pattern and rhythm of each book had to be invaded. I often felt a trespasser on sacred ground as I hunted through the poems in *Above the River*, but despite this response, I persevered and made choices.

It wasn't difficult to choose old favorites or poems in honor of family and certain friends, but it was hard, sometimes painful, to pick and then reject poems that had special and personal meaning for me. I always had to keep in mind how the book must appear as a whole.

When I met and married James in 1967, he had almost completed *Shall We Gather at the River*. Most of those poems had been written before I knew him. He typed out one of the last poems, "The Lights in the Hallway," and sent it to me from the Hotel Regent, where he lived during the early part of his life in New York. I used to carry it in my purse to read on the bus as I went back and forth to my job. It was natural for me to gravitate to the later books, especially those written after our first trip to Europe in 1970. It was then that the darkness in his poems became infused with the light of Italy and France. And just as I was more involved with the later books, Robert was, perhaps, more involved with the earlier books, especially *The Branch Will Not Break*.

The poet Campbell McGrath expressed my own feelings about James's later work in "A Letter to James Wright," from his book *Road Atlas*:

> . . . I love so many of those last poems, treasure them like sacral beings, a flowering of such magnitude near the end of a difficult life, as if the pear tree that stood for years unclothed in the rain and snow of Ohio had at the last, unbidden, blossomed.

> But we are not trees and it requires an act of will for us to bloom

> and it is the courage of that action I admire,

> the willingness to recreate your art anew . . .

> the strength to persevere and the gift of change . . .

During the spring and summer of 2000, Robert worked in Minnesota and I in Rhode Island trying to put together our selections. When we exchanged our personal lists of about eighty poems, we discovered only forty-four of them were the same.

We were in luck, though. Galway Kinnell, an excellent friend and poet, had agreed to act as a consultant for us. Robert sent him a list of the forty-four poems upon which we had agreed, as well as lists of our separate choices. Galway, with the forty-four poems as a base, worked only with the titles of the personal lists and came up with a book of seventy-two poems. Robert and I added ten more, and the book was complete.

As coeditor, I feel most fortunate in working with Robert, who was always sensitive to and considerate of my whims and wishes. I am deeply grateful to Galway for his wisdom and generous gift of time. Jonathan Blunk, James's authorized biographer, spent many hours proofreading and correcting typographical errors from earlier editions, for which I am deeply appreciative. This was a harmonious and happy undertaking, carried out in a spirit that I feel James would both approve and appreciate.

I greatly admired an exhibit of manuscripts curated by Rodney Philips at the New York Public Library on Forty-second Street in 1995, titled "The Hand of the Poet." Included was some of James's work, and in a companion book published with the same title I found these words especially compelling:

> Wright would often return, if only in spirit, to Ohio and to his childhood for themes and context for his poetry . . . his voice became one of the sweetest of the age, his great subject the heart's passage to the deepest interior consciousness, to the moment of perfect awareness, of pure being and of pure enlightenment.

As I worked on this book, I certainly felt the respect and love both Robert and Galway have for James, his poetry and his spirit. It was almost as if James himself had been with us.

Anne Wright

## Introduction: James Wright's Clarity and Extravagance
by Robert Bly

In great poets we often find a calmness and undisturbed beauty, a serenity and a clarity. Li Po said:

> If you were to ask me why I dwell among green mountains,
> I should laugh silently; my soul is serene.
> The peach blossom follows the moving water;
> There is another heaven and earth beyond the world of men.
>
> *(translated by Robert Payne)*

The poem becomes transparent. The Latin word associated with this quality is *claritas*. It's good to taste of this clear heaven, to bring it close to your chest, to experience it in youth before trouble, illness, poverty fall on you, and the dark times come.

In James Wright's early poems, we meet a master of *claritas*. To some extent, he learned it from his teacher, John Crowe Ransom, whose prose and poetry shine with a consistent serenity that never fades. Wright learned *claritas* as well from the poems of Po Chu-i and Li Po, which Robert Payne gathered in *The White Pony*, published in 1947.

Wright wrote a poem called "Three Steps to the Graveyard," which was published in his first book. This is the final stanza:

> O now as I go there
> The crowfoot, the mayapple
> Blear the gray pond;
> Beside the still waters
> The field mouse tiptoes,
> To hear the air sounding
> The long hollow thorn.

I lean to the hollow,
But nothing blows there,
The day goes down.
The field mice flutter
Like grass and are gone,
And a skinny old woman
Scrubs at a stone,
Between two trees.

Transparency and lightheartedness can be intensified by a careful (if apparently careless) repeating of musical notes; we can feel these notes often in Whitman's poems.

Wright deepens the *claritas* by carefully singling out and repeating certain vowels. In this final stanza, *oh* occurs ten times, *ee* is repeated four times, and *ay* three times. The phoneme *er* repeats eight times, and so on. When we take in the poem, it is as if we see into a meadow through brilliant windows of sound.

*Claritas* brings an inner shining. The language is transparent as water in a pool, dignified, shining from inside, clairvoyant, undisturbed, ecstatic. Juan Ramón Jiménez says:

—My beloved is only water,
that always passes away, and does not deceive,
that always passes away, and does not change,
that always passes away, and does not end.

*(translated by James Wright)*

Jiménez stayed in shining all his life. Po Chu-i did the same; Wallace Stevens and Wisława Szymborska are faithful to it. When poets remain in *claritas* all their life, Federico García Lorca delightedly calls them "angels."

In "My Grandmother's Ghost," published in 1957, Wright imagines her ghost slipping over a shallow river and fluttering up a path:

Even before she reached the empty house,
She beat her wings ever so lightly, rose,
Followed a bee where apples blew like snow;
And then, forgetting what she wanted there,
Too full of blossom and green light to care,
She hurried to the ground, and slipped below.

James Wright didn't remain an "angel" all his life, so what was his route? He took a deep breath and went down.

My name is James A. Wright, and I was born
Twenty-five miles from this infected grave,
In Martins Ferry, Ohio, where one slave
To Hazel-Atlas Glass became my father.

The infected grave he mentions refers to the spot where a murderer named George Doty was buried by the State. Wright's poem "At the Executed Murderer's Grave," published in *Saint Judas* in 1959, is confusing and confused: the author insists that he himself is a liar and partly mad ("I run like the bewildered mad / at St. Clair Sanitarium"). We can say that this poem opens the second stage of his work. He agrees to his own shame and guilt. Perhaps his guilt will heal "when every man stands still / By the last sea." He gives us for the first time the curious mix of honesty, hostility, and bravado that will be his mood in many new poems:

Order be damned, I do not want to die,
Even to keep Belaire, Ohio, safe.

The revelation of fear and sorrow continues in dozens of poems, including those in *The Branch Will Not Break*, a title that, of course, implies it may break. On the flyleaf of my copy of *The Branch*, he wrote, "Let us hope the precious herbs will really be found."

*The Branch Will Not Break* begins with a poem that is set not in Ohio but in ancient China. It is called "As I Step Over a Puddle at the End of Winter, I Think of an Ancient Chinese Governor." There is a change here from his early poems, not only in mood but in language habits; he no longer fills out the line with reassuring literary language. The second line ends abruptly after three words:

Po Chu-i, balding old politician,
What's the use?
I think of you,
Uneasily entering the gorges of the Yang-Tze,
When you were being towed up the rapids
Toward some political job or other
In the city of Chungshou.
You made it, I guess,
By dark.

But it is 1960, it is almost spring again,
And the tall rocks of Minneapolis
Build me my own black twilight
Of bamboo ropes and waters.
Where is Yuan Chen, the friend you loved?
Where is the sea, that once solved the whole loneliness
Of the Midwest? Where is Minneapolis? I can see nothing
But the great terrible oak tree darkening with winter.
Did you find the city of isolated men beyond mountains?
Or have you been holding the end of a frayed rope
For a thousand years?

The poem is just as subtle and intimate as the lighthearted early poems, but we can feel the adult fatigue—"being towed up the rapids / Toward some political job or other"—and room is left in the poem for depression, exasperation, and sorrow. Perhaps the most important presence is a failure that can't be blamed on anyone else. The last image—of a man holding the end of a frayed rope for a thousand years—does express this failure, even if there were no other images in the poem.

If Wright were a painter, we would say that dark brown, purple, and black have entered his palette. One impatient critic calculated that the words *dark, darkness,* and *darkening* appear more than forty times in the twenty-six pages that *The Branch Will Not Break* occupies in the *Collected Poems.* A fellow poet, Robert Hass, who greatly admires Wright's work, was exasperated by Wright's constant emphasis on shadowy material. Hass pointed to these lines from the poem "On Minding One's Own Business" in *Saint Judas*:

From prudes and muddying fools,
Kind Aphrodite, spare
All hunted criminals,
Hoboes, and whip-poor-wills,
And girls with rumpled hair . . .

None of these shadowy beings is Apollonian; they all share in the metaphorical dark. Hass worried that Wright was suffering from some sort of cultural disease, perhaps typical of the sixties, in which everything dark was good. He expressed the fear that if Wright—or any poet—began to celebrate the dark, the unlucky poet would stray into the confused and undifferentiated, and pull literature in after him. He would lose his ability to distinguish between light and dark. On the other side, we notice that the alchemists honored the "massa confusa" and began their search there for the glory of the universe.

This turn toward the darkness in Wright's poetry did become persistent. In the *Branch Will Not Break* poems, it is clear that the shadow has become as nourishing as the light once was in his crowfoot and mayapple poems:

My face is turned away from the sun.
A horse grazes in my long shadow.

The doubts that many critics expressed about Wright's direction doubled and redoubled when he published "Lying in a Hammock at William Duffy's Farm in Pine Island, Minnesota." The title is a playful acknowledgment of the elaborate titles that classical Chinese poets gave to their poems. We could say the poem moves in a way well known in old Chinese poems, but the last line is definitely American:

Over my head, I see the bronze butterfly,
Asleep on the black trunk,
Blowing like a leaf in green shadow.
Down the ravine behind the empty house,
The cowbells follow one another
Into the distances of the afternoon.
To my right,
In a field of sunlight between two pines,
The droppings of last year's horses
Blaze up into golden stones.
I lean back, as the evening darkens and comes on.
A chicken hawk floats over, looking for home.
I have wasted my life.

Many people love the marvels of this poem, right up to the chicken hawk. But it is the last line that drove critics mad, and still does. When he has written such beautiful poems, how can he even suggest he has wasted his life! What can one say? The abruptness of the last line efficiently pulls the poem from the angel category. He says, "I'll fix this poem so you can't put it in an anthology of angel poems." One might add that he knows that the images in the poem are marvelous and are testimonies to the glory of the universe, but it's also true that he has lost much of his life precisely by devoting himself to such marvelous images. The miracle takes place even if no poet notices it; the universe itself arranges for horse droppings to blaze up in the afternoon sun, and for trees to show a black trunk with a bronze butterfly on it. What seems easy for the universe is often hard for us. Many readers wanted the poem to remain conventionally positive to the very last syllable. It didn't. Ed Ochester has also mentioned that Wright's longing for home was so intense at this moment in his life that as soon as he set down the chicken hawk line ending with the word *home*, his own life looked desolate to him.

Wright spent a lot of time in *Saint Judas* describing the ruined landscape around the Ohio River. In "Stages on a Journey Westward," published in 1963, he checks to see how the rest of the country is doing. In western Minnesota he notices:

> The only human beings between me and the Pacific Ocean
> Were old Indians, who wanted to kill me.

This is a reasonable paranoia. These are the words of a grandson of immigrants noticing that his ancestors did not win the continent fairly. In part four, James finally arrives at the Pacific:

> Defeated for re-election,
> The half-educated sheriff of Mukilteo, Washington,
> Has been drinking again.
> He leads me up the cliff, tottering.
> Both drunk, we stand among the graves.
> Miners paused here on the way up to Alaska.
> Angry, they spaded their broken women's bodies
> Into ditches of crab grass.
> I lie down between tombstones.
> At the bottom of the cliff
> America is over and done with.
> America,
> Plunged into the dark furrows
> Of the sea again.

We've been reading Wright's poems of darkness, which amount to a new stage. The "dark" poems lack some of the elegance of the poems in the stage of clarity, but they bring in depth and fierceness. In any case, Wright was himself living the dark. About the time he was writing these poems, Allen Tate took part in the refusal to give him tenure at the University of Minnesota, which had the effect of driving him deeper into the darkness. He had been teaching at the university for six years, but as a specialist in Dickens and a general lecturer in literature. Wright got a temporary job teaching at Macalester College in St. Paul for two years, but hostile letters Tate placed in his dossier prevented his getting a real job elsewhere. When lead after lead dried up, James said to me, "Robert, I am never going to get a job again. I'm never going to be loved by a woman again either." He suffered several serious breakdowns during that time. He was assigned an English doctor, Dr. Lamb, who liked shock treatments and gave Jim a number of them. When Jim's wife came to see him, he gave her a shock treatment as well. The marriage broke up; subsequently Wright lost any close association with his two sons. His drinking got worse.

> America is over and done with.
> America,
> Plunged into the dark furrows
> Of the sea again.

This travel from transparency to darkness is like traveling from one island to another. The cost is high for a writer who travels from the first island to the second. There is a big difference between *All's Well That Ends Well* and *Macbeth*. Sometimes the second stage means breakdowns, but on the other hand, as Ezra Pound remarked, one doesn't get through hell in a hurry. T. S. Eliot, who had to give up a lot of self-esteem, remarked, when asked if a life of hell was worth it for the sake of the poem, "No." Pablo Neruda, at that stage in his life, said:

It so happens I am sick of being a man.
And it happens that I walk into tailorshops and movie houses
dried up, waterproof, like a swan made of felt
steering my way in a water of wombs and ashes. . . .

It so happens I am sick of my feet and my nails
and my hair and my shadow.
It so happens I am sick of being a man.

Still it would be marvelous
to terrify a law clerk with a cut lily,
or kill a nun with a blow on the ear. . . .

*(translated by Robert Bly)*

César Vallejo said:

Well, on the day I was born,
God was sick.

They all know that I'm alive,
that I'm vicious; and they don't know
the December that follows from that January.
Well, on the day I was born,
God was sick.

*(translated by James Wright)*

Years earlier Wright had found Georg Trakl, who wrote, in Wright's
translation:

The white walls of the city are always giving off sound.
Under arching thorns
O my brother blind minute-hands we are climbing toward mid-
night.

Wright published in 1977 a remarkable poem called "Hook," which I'll set down here:

I was only a young man
In those days. On that evening
The cold was so God damned
Bitter there was nothing.
Nothing. I was in trouble
With a woman, and there was nothing
There but me and dead snow.

I stood on the street corner
In Minneapolis, lashed
This way and that.
Wind rose from some pit,
Hunting me.
Another bus to Saint Paul
Would arrive in three hours,
If I was lucky.

Then the young Sioux
Loomed beside me, his scars
Were just my age.

Ain't got no bus here
A long time, he said.
You got enough money
To get home on?

What did they do
To your hand? I answered.
He raised up his hook into the terrible starlight
And slashed the wind.

Oh, that? he said.
I had a bad time with a woman. Here,
You take this.

Did you ever feel a man hold
Sixty-five cents
In a hook,
And place it
Gently
In your freezing hand?

I took it.
It wasn't the money I needed.
But I took it.

Here the emotion is carried not by clear, open vowels but by short, awkward language particles, *k*'s and *t*'s. Wright could have said to the Sioux man, "I'm all right. You keep it." But in the phrase "I took it," we can feel both desperation and compassion; he accepts his position as one of the low ones of earth; all of the elevation he had gained through language is gone.

A poem is only a poem; *scar* and *hook* are only words; but before or under them are years of difficult living. We've talked about the first and second acts in the life of a poet. It's possible Wright's late poems from Italy represent a third act.

These poems are set mostly in Padua, Verona, and the hill cities of Tuscany, where he felt the culture of Saint Francis, Giotto, Catullus, and Cimabue. He experienced the presence of beauty more deeply in these cities than in the towns around Martins Ferry, and since it was always for beauty that Wright lived, it seems right that his poems would settle finally in Tuscany.

Wright's mode of writing changes now from restless moments of beauty interspersed with brutal truth-telling, to a complicated poetry of gratitude. Remembering that Virgil had said, *"Optima dies*

*prima fugit"*—"The best days go first"—he writes, speaking of a bee
caught in a ripe pear, which he has released with a knife:

> The bee shuddered, and returned.
> Maybe I should have left him alone there,
> Drowning in his own delight.
> The best days are the first
> To flee, sang the lovely
> Musician born in this town
> So like my own.

At the end of "Butterfly Fish," he remarks that this little fish

> . . . grazes up his tall corals,
> Slim as a stallion, serene on his far-off hillside,
> His other world where I cannot see
> His secret face.

By this time he has quit drinking and is stronger than before.
Speaking of sumac, he says:

> The skin will turn aside hatchets and knife blades . . .

In "The Secret of Light," he says:

> I am startled to discover that I am not afraid. I am free to
> give a blessing out of my silence into that woman's black
> hair. I trust her to go on living. I believe in her black hair,
> her diamond that is still asleep. I would close my eyes to
> daydream about her. But those silent companions who
> watch over me from the insides of my eyelids are too bril-
> liant for me to meet face to face.

In "The Silent Angel," we have the feeling that he is doing more seeing than he has for a long time:

> . . . and all I could see behind me were the diminishing cicadas, lindens, and slim cedars rising, one feather folding upwards into another, into the spaces of evergreen and gold beyond the Roman Arena . . .

In the town of Sirmione ("Piccolini"), he sees:

> An easy thousand of silver, almost transparent piccolini are skimming the surface of the long slab of volcanic stone.

In "The Silent Angel," he praises a musician he has seen in Verona:

> He just waved me as gently as he could on the way out. . . . And he did his best, I suppose. He owns that heavenly city no more than I do. He may be fallen, as I am. But from a greater height, unless I miss my guess.

The language tends to be sweet, airy, and extravagant. Wright says in "The Gift of Change":

> But the lizard lying beside me now has gone too far. Wholly abandoning himself to his gift of change, he lifts his head above the edge of a linden blossom freshly fallen and alone. His exquisite hands have given up clinging to anything. They lie open. The leaf on the flower is so smooth, a light wind could blow him away. I wonder if he knows. If he knows, I wonder that my breath doesn't blow him away. I am that close to him, and he that close to me. He has gone too far into the world to turn back now.

It's interesting that as Wright adapted his language to the prose poem, he asked it to convey this new mood of praise. Stephen Yenser—who has written a marvelous essay on Wright's late poems, "Open Secrets," in *James Wright: The Heart of the Light* (edited by Peter Stitt and Frank Graziano)—remarks, speaking of *Moments of the Italian Summer*: "Its fourteen prose poems . . . are as transparent as anything he has written, though they are shot through with whimsy. In fact, in the best of them, extravagance provides coherence and sophistication alike."

If we compare these prose poems to "My Grandmother's Ghost" and the mayapple poem, we see Wright prepared for forgiveness. In the third act we see an intelligence like that of Prospero's looking back on a life of many errors but admiring the mysterious wholeness of it all. Moreover, we could say—even though the comparison may be a bit presumptuous—that we don't get to *The Tempest* without going through *King Lear* and *Macbeth*.

Yenser says, "Wright's version of the prose poem, with its evident tolerance for loose ends, its appetite for digression, its fugitive unity, seems exactly the form to contain [the journal passages] without warping them." Yenser continues, "What happens in such pieces is that the bud of the actual blossoms into the extravagant flower of vision."

Wright says of a turtle ("The Turtle Overnight"):

. . . It was as near as I've ever come to seeing a turtle take a pleasant bath in his natural altogether. All the legendary faces of broken old age disappeared from my mind, the thickened muscles under the chins, the nostrils brutal with hatred, the murdering eyes. He filled my mind with a sweet-tasting mountain rain, his youthfulness, his modesty as he washed himself all alone, his religious face.

And in a poem set in Fiesole ("The Art of the Fugue: A Prayer"), he says:

And me there a long way from the cold dream of Hell.
Me, there, alone, at last,
At last with the dust of my dust,
As far away as I will ever get from dying,
And the two great poets of God in the silence
Meeting together.

He means Bach and Dante. Late in his life, the mathematician
William Hamilton said, "When thinking as a mathematician, hu-
man bodies, emotions, and interpersonal relationships take on less
and less importance, whereas the universe as an expression of num-
ber relationships takes on more and more. There are ecstatic mo-
ments." I think the important word is *universe*. The honor is not
given to human beings, but to the universe.

Wright says in "To the Creature of the Creation":

Lonely as my desire is,
I have no daughter.
I will not die by fire, I
Shall die by water.

By this time he had worked for years as a highly valued teacher at
Hunter College in New York City. He had met and married Annie.
He had taken part in a sweet concord. They had become a pair.
With her, he could praise the sweetness of a deep culture still some-
how existent. In this passage from "A Winter Daybreak Above
Vence," he mentions the pleasure of a visit to a fellow poet, Galway
Kinnell, and his wife:

. . . The moon and the stars
Suddenly flicker out, and the whole mountain
Appears, pale as a shell.

Look, the sea has not fallen and broken
Our heads. How can I feel so warm
Here in the dead center of January? I can
Scarcely believe it, and yet I have to, this is
The only life I have. I get up from the stone.
My body mumbles something unseemly
And follows me. Now we are all sitting here strangely
On top of the sunlight.

James Wright had an immense love of literature, and he memorized vast quantities of it. One night, after a reading at a local university, a member of the English department, apparently annoyed by remarks about iambic meter, suggested that Wright knew nothing about English literature. He responded by reciting the entire last chapter of *Tristram Shandy* by heart. Wright had good teachers at Kenyon College and in Seattle. He enlisted in the army in June 1946, after the war was over; the GI Bill made a good education possible. He was born into a generation that had seen many men their age die in battle, and he was determined to sacrifice something himself for those dead. He loved being with bike riders and drinkers in Minneapolis bars, and he was capable of feeling the suffering "of the bewildered mad." All of these enthusiasms added to his intensity, but in the end it is his power as a verbal alchemist and his truth-telling that hold his readers close to him.

Wright railed at the United States as a way of gaining its attention, to see if the United States could defend itself and express what it stood for. He didn't lie to himself about the enormous defects in American culture or the banality of its cities:

And nobody would commit suicide, only
To find beyond death
Bridgeport, Ohio.

He never gave up his fellowship with the condemned. He wouldn't have been surprised that the governor of Illinois recently released to the ordinary prison a number of men on death row because the judicial system has so many flaws in it. The longing for justice is at the very center of his poems.

What else did Wright want? He wanted clear language; he wanted to get rid of the clutter of language in the American poetry of his time. Speaking about the year he spent in occupied Japan just after World War II, he wrote that he was able in Japan "to conceive of a poem as something which, with the greatest modesty, is brought up close to its subject so that it can be suggestive and evocative. Japan was a revelation to me." He achieved that closeness in a number of poems, among them "A Blessing."

He wanted less attention to deathless abstractions such as democracy, freedom, and Christianity and more honoring of actual creatures that live and die. In "From a Bus Window in Central Ohio, Just Before a Thunder Shower," he says:

Cribs loaded with roughage huddle together
Before the north clouds.
The wind tiptoes between poplars.
The silver maple leaves squint
Toward the ground.
An old farmer, his scarlet face
Apologetic with whiskey, swings back a barn door
And calls a hundred black-and-white Holsteins
From the clover field.

When LeRoi Jones wrote Jim a blistering letter about this poem, ending with a sarcastic question, "How did you know there were a hundred Holsteins?" Jim was not rattled. He understood that he was being attacked as a foolish praiser of nature. He wrote a postcard back that said, "I counted the tits and divided by four. Yours sincerely, James Wright."

What more did Jim Wright want from poetry? He wanted truth-telling and passion. It was rather cruel of him to ask for that from America in the late fifties, almost as cruel as asking for it now.

As for passion, it implies staking a lot on one throw, all or nothing. He referred in his poems several times to a woman who had drowned in the river; in "To the Muse," published in 1968, he says:

> Come up to me, love,
> Out of the river, or I will
> Come down to you.

Wright doesn't suggest that it's easy to live your life in poetry:

> It is all right. All they do
> Is go in by dividing
> One rib from another. I wouldn't
> Lie to you. It hurts
> Like nothing I know. All they do
> Is burn their way in with a wire. . . .

> Three lady doctors in Wheeling open
> Their offices at night.
> I don't have to call them, they are always there.
> But they only have to put the knife once
> Under your breast.
> Then they hang their contraption.
> And you bear it.

Why are James Wright's poems so good? Besides his truth-telling, his grief, and his affections, he has genius in language. His gift has something to do with the interstices between words, the mysterious events that happen when simple words are placed next to one another, as in "Milkweed":

. . . At a touch of my hand,
The air fills with delicate creatures
From the other world.

I'll end with his poem "In Memory of Leopardi." We see an amazing variety of nouns—barbs, oblivions, lame prayers, smoke marrow, hunchbacks, even invented adjectives such as "jubilating Isaiah." Wright's genius shows in the touches of surprise, in the drawing upon an immense vocabulary, in the drawing down of words by some part of the brain far from daylight consciousness, far from reason:

I have gone past all those times when the poets
Were beautiful as only
The rich can be. The cold bangles
Of the moon grazed one of my shoulders,
And so to this day,
And beyond, I carry
The sliver of a white city, the barb of a jewel
In my left clavicle that hunches.
Tonight I sling
A scrambling sack of oblivions and lame prayers
On my right good arm. The Ohio River
Has flown by me twice, the dark jubilating
Isaiah of mill and smoke marrow. Blind son
Of a meadow of huge horses, lover of drowned islands
Above Steubenville, blind father
Of my halt gray wing:
Now I limp on, knowing
The moon strides behind me, swinging
The scimitar of the divinity that struck down
The hunchback in agony
When he saw her, naked, carrying away his last sheep
Through the Asian rocks.

# Selected Poems

## Sitting in a Small Screenhouse on a Summer Morning

Ten more miles, it is South Dakota.
Somehow, the roads there turn blue,
When no one walks down them.
One more night of walking, and I could have become
A horse, a blue horse, dancing
Down a road, alone.

I have got this far. It is almost noon. But never mind time:
That is all over.
It is still Minnesota.
Among a few dead cornstalks, the starving shadow
Of a crow leaps to his death.
At least, it is green here,
Although between my body and the elder trees
A savage hornet strains at the wire screen.
He can't get in yet.

It is so still now, I hear the horse
Clear his nostrils.
He has crept out of the green places behind me.
Patient and affectionate, he reads over my shoulder
These words I have written.
He has lived a long time, and he loves to pretend
No one can see him.
Last night I paused at the edge of darkness,
And slept with green dew, alone.
I have come a long way, to surrender my shadow
To the shadow of a horse.

from

# The Green Wall

## Three Steps to the Graveyard

When I went there first,
In the spring, it was evening,
It was long hollow thorn
Laid under the locust,
And near to my feet
The crowfoot, the mayapple
Trod their limbs down
Till the stalk blew over.
It grew summer, O riches
Of girls on the lawn,
And boys' locks lying
Tousled on knees,
The picnickers leaving,
The day gone down.

When I went there again,
I walked with my father
Who held in his hand
The crowfoot, the mayapple,
And under my hands,
To hold off the sunlight,
I saw him going,
Between two trees;
When the lawn lay empty
It was the year's end,
It was the darkness,
It was long hollow thorn
To wound the bare shade,
The sheaf and the blade.

O now as I go there
The crowfoot, the mayapple
Blear the gray pond;
Beside the still waters
The field mouse tiptoes,
To hear the air sounding
The long hollow thorn.
I lean to the hollow,
But nothing blows there,
The day goes down.
The field mice flutter
Like grass and are gone,
And a skinny old woman
Scrubs at a stone,
Between two trees.

## Father

In paradise I poised my foot above the boat and said:
Who prayed for me?
                              But only the dip of an oar
In water sounded; slowly fog from some cold shore
Circled in wreaths around my head.

But who is waiting?
                              And the wind began,
Transfiguring my face from nothingness
To tiny weeping eyes. And when my voice
Grew real, there was a place
Far, far below on earth. There was a tiny man—

It was my father wandering round the waters at the wharf.
Irritably he circled and he called
Out to the marine currents up and down,
But heard only a cold unmeaning cough,
And saw the oarsman in the mist enshawled.

He drew me from the boat. I was asleep.
And we went home together.

# A Song for the Middle of the Night

By way of explaining to my son the following curse by
Eustace Deschamps: "Happy is he who has no children;
for babies bring nothing but crying and stench."


Now first of all he means the night
  You beat the crib and cried
And brought me spinning out of bed
  To powder your backside.
I rolled your buttocks over
  And I could not complain:
Legs up, la la, legs down, la la,
  Back to sleep again.

Now second of all he means the day
  You dabbled out of doors
And dragged a dead cat Billy-be-damned
  Across the kitchen floors.
I rolled your buttocks over
  And made you sing for pain:
Legs up, la la, legs down, la la,
  Back to sleep again.

But third of all my father once
  Laid me across his knee
And solved the trouble when he beat
  The yowling out of me.
He rocked me on his shoulder
  When razor straps were vain:
Legs up, la la, legs down, la la,
  Back to sleep again.

So roll upon your belly, boy,
    And bother being cursed.
You turn the household upside down,
    But you are not the first.
Deschamps the poet blubbered too,
    For all his fool disdain:
Legs up, la la, legs down, la la,
    Back to sleep again.

## To a Hostess Saying Good Night

Shake out the ruffle, turn and go,
Over the trellis blow the kiss.
Some of the guests will never know
Another night to shadow this.
Some of the birds awake in vines
Will never see another face
So frail, so lovely anyplace
Between the birdbath and the bines.

O dark come never down to you.
I look away and look away:
Over the moon the shadows go,
Over your shoulder, nebulae.
Some of the vast, the vacant stars
Will never see your face at all,
Your frail, your lovely eyelids fall
Between Andromeda and Mars.

# Mutterings over the Crib of a Deaf Child

"How will he hear the bell at school
Arrange the broken afternoon,
And know to run across the cool
Grasses where the starlings cry,
Or understand the day is gone?"

Well, someone lifting curious brows
Will take the measure of the clock.
And he will see the birchen boughs
Outside sagging dark from the sky,
And the shade crawling upon the rock.

"And how will he know to rise at morning?
His mother has other sons to waken,
She has the stove she must build to burning
Before the coals of the nighttime die;
And he never stirs when he is shaken."

I take it the air affects the skin,
And you remember, when you were young,
Sometimes you could feel the dawn begin,
And the fire would call you, by and by,
Out of the bed and bring you along.

"Well, good enough. To serve his needs
All kinds of arrangements can be made.
But what will you do if his finger bleeds?
Or a bobwhite whistles invisibly
And flutes like an angel off in the shade?"

He will learn pain. And, as for the bird,
It is always darkening when that comes out.
I will putter as though I had not heard,
And lift him into my arms and sing
Whether he hears my song or not.

# My Grandmother's Ghost

She skimmed the yellow water like a moth,
Trailing her feet across the shallow stream;
She saw the berries, paused and sampled them
Where a slight spider cleaned his narrow tooth.
Light in the air, she fluttered up the path,
So delicate to shun the leaves and damp,
Like some young wife, holding a slender lamp
To find her stray child, or the moon, or both.

Even before she reached the empty house,
She beat her wings ever so lightly, rose,
Followed a bee where apples blew like snow;
And then, forgetting what she wanted there,
Too full of blossom and green light to care,
She hurried to the ground, and slipped below.

from

# Saint Judas

## Complaint

She's gone. She was my love, my moon or more.
She chased the chickens out and swept the floor,
Emptied the bones and nut-shells after feasts,
And smacked the kids for leaping up like beasts.
Now morbid boys have grown past awkwardness;
The girls let stitches out, dress after dress,
To free some swinging body's riding space
And form the new child's unimagined face.
Yet, while vague nephews, spitting on their curls,
Amble to pester winds and blowsy girls,
What arm will sweep the room, what hand will hold
New snow against the milk to keep it cold?
And who will dump the garbage, feed the hogs,
And pitch the chickens' heads to hungry dogs?
Not my lost hag who dumbly bore such pain:
Childbirth and midnight sassafras and rain.
New snow against her face and hands she bore,
And now lies down, who was my moon or more.

# An Offering for Mr. Bluehart

That was a place, when I was young,
Where two or three good friends and I
Tested the fruit against the tongue
Or threw the withered windfalls by.
The sparrows, angry in the sky,
Denounced us from a broken bough.
They limp along the wind and die.
The apples all are eaten now.

Behind the orchard, past one hill
The lean satanic owner lay
And threatened us with murder till
We stole his riches all away.
He caught us in the act one day
And damned us to the laughing bone,
And fired his gun across the gray
Autumn where now his life is done.

Sorry for him, or any man
Who lost his labored wealth to thieves,
Today I mourn him, as I can,
By leaving in their golden leaves
Some luscious apples overhead.
Now may my abstinence restore
Peace to the orchard and the dead.
We shall not nag them any more.

# A Note Left in Jimmy Leonard's Shack

Near the dry river's water-mark we found
    Your brother Minnegan,
Flopped like a fish against the muddy ground.
Beany, the kid whose yellow hair turns green,
Told me to find you, even in the rain,
    And tell you he was drowned.

I hid behind the chassis on the bank,
    The wreck of someone's Ford:
I was afraid to come and wake you drunk:
You told me once the waking up was hard,
The daylight beating at you like a board.
    Blood in my stomach sank.

Besides, you told him never to go out
    Along the river-side
Drinking and singing, clattering about.
You might have thrown a rock at me and cried
I was to blame, I let him fall in the road
    And pitch down on his side.

Well, I'll get hell enough when I get home
    For coming up this far,
Leaving the note, and running as I came.
I'll go and tell my father where you are.
You'd better go find Minnegan before
    Policemen hear and come.

Beany went home, and I got sick and ran,
    You old son of a bitch.
You better hurry down to Minnegan;
He's drunk or dying now, I don't know which,
Rolled in the roots and garbage like a fish,
    The poor old man.

# A Breath of Air

I walked, when love was gone,
Out of the human town,
For an easy breath of air.
Beyond a break in the trees,
Beyond the hangdog lives
Of old men, beyond girls:
The tall stars held their peace.
Looking in vain for lies
I turned, like earth, to go.
An owl's wings hovered, bare
On the moon's hills of snow.

And things were as they were.

## But Only Mine

I dreamed that I was dead, as all men do,
And feared the dream, though hardly for the sake
Of any thrust of pain my flesh might take
Below the softening shales. Bereft of you,
I lay for days and days alone, I knew
Somewhere above me boughs were burning gold,
And women's frocks were loose, and men grew old.

Grew old. And shrivelled. Asked the time of day.
And then forgot. Turned. Looked among the grass.
Tripped on a twig. Frightened some leaves away.
Children. And girls. I knew, above my face,
Rabbit and jay flocked, wondering how to cross
An empty field stripped naked to the sun.
They halted into a shadow, huddled down.

Rabbit and jay, old man, and girl, and child,
All moved above me, dreaming of broad light.
I heard you walking through the empty field.
Startled awake, I found my living sight:
The grave drifted away, and it was night,
I felt your soft despondent shoulders near.
Out of my dream, the dead rose everywhere.

I did not dream your death, but only mine.

# At the Executed Murderer's Grave

*for J. L. D.*

Why should we do this? What good is it to us? Above all, how
can we do such a thing? How can it possibly be done?

—Freud

1

My name is James A. Wright, and I was born
Twenty-five miles from this infected grave,
In Martins Ferry, Ohio, where one slave
To Hazel-Atlas Glass became my father.
He tried to teach me kindness. I return
Only in memory now, aloof, unhurried,
To dead Ohio, where I might lie buried,
Had I not run away before my time.
Ohio caught George Doty. Clean as lime,
His skull rots empty here. Dying's the best
Of all the arts men learn in a dead place.
I walked here once. I made my loud display,
Leaning for language on a dead man's voice.
Now sick of lies, I turn to face the past.
I add my easy grievance to the rest:

2

Doty, if I confess I do not love you,
Will you let me alone? I burn for my own lies.
The nights electrocute my fugitive,
My mind. I run like the bewildered mad
At St. Clair Sanitarium, who lurk,
Arch and cunning, under the maple trees,
Pleased to be playing guilty after dark.

Staring to bed, they croon self-lullabies.
Doty, you make me sick. I am not dead.
I croon my tears at fifty cents per line.


3
Idiot, he demanded love from girls,
And murdered one. Also, he was a thief.
He left two women, and a ghost with child.
The hair, foul as a dog's upon his head,
Made such revolting Ohio animals
Fitter for vomit than a kind man's grief.
I waste no pity on the dead that stink,
And no love's lost between me and the crying
Drunks of Belaire, Ohio, where police
Kick at their kidneys till they die of drink.
Christ may restore them whole, for all of me.
Alive and dead, those giggling muckers who
Saddled my nightmares thirty years ago
Can do without my widely printed sighing
Over their pains with paid sincerity.
I do not pity the dead, I pity the dying.


4
I pity myself, because a man is dead.
If Belmont County killed him, what of me?
His victims never loved him. Why should we?
And yet, nobody had to kill him either.
It does no good to woo the grass, to veil
The quicklime hole of a man's defeat and shame.
Nature-lovers are gone. To hell with them.
I kick the clods away, and speak my name.

5

This grave's gash festers. Maybe it will heal,
When all are caught with what they had to do
In fear of love, when every man stands still
By the last sea,
And the princes of the sea come down
To lay away their robes, to judge the earth
And its dead, and we dead stand undefended everywhere,
And my bodies—father and child and unskilled criminal—
Ridiculously kneel to bare my scars,
My sneaking crimes, to God's unpitying stars.


6

Staring politely, they will not mark my face
From any murderer's, buried in this place.
Why should they? We are nothing but a man.


7

Doty, the rapist and the murderer,
Sleeps in a ditch of fire, and cannot hear;
And where, in earth or hell's unholy peace,
Men's suicides will stop, God knows, not I.
Angels and pebbles mock me under trees.
Earth is a door I cannot even face.
Order be damned, I do not want to die,
Even to keep Belaire, Ohio, safe.
The hackles on my neck are fear, not grief.
(Open, dungeon! Open, roof of the ground!)
I hear the last sea in the Ohio grass,
Heaving a tide of gray disastrousness.
Wrinkles of winter ditch the rotted face
Of Doty, killer, imbecile, and thief:
Dirt of my flesh, defeated, underground.

## Saint Judas

When I went out to kill myself, I caught
A pack of hoodlums beating up a man.
Running to spare his suffering, I forgot
My name, my number, how my day began,
How soldiers milled around the garden stone
And sang amusing songs; how all that day
Their javelins measured crowds; how I alone
Bargained the proper coins, and slipped away.

Banished from heaven, I found this victim beaten,
Stripped, kneed, and left to cry. Dropping my rope
Aside, I ran, ignored the uniforms:
Then I remembered bread my flesh had eaten,
The kiss that ate my flesh. Flayed without hope,
I held the man for nothing in my arms.

from

# The Branch Will Not Break

# As I Step over a Puddle at the End of Winter, I Think of an Ancient Chinese Governor

And how can I, born in evil days
And fresh from failure, ask a kindness of Fate?
                    —Written A.D. 819


Po Chu-i, balding old politician,
What's the use?
I think of you,
Uneasily entering the gorges of the Yang-Tze,
When you were being towed up the rapids
Toward some political job or other
In the city of Chungshou.
You made it, I guess,
By dark.

But it is 1960, it is almost spring again,
And the tall rocks of Minneapolis
Build me my own black twilight
Of bamboo ropes and waters.
Where is Yuan Chen, the friend you loved?
Where is the sea, that once solved the whole loneliness
Of the Midwest? Where is Minneapolis? I can see nothing
But the great terrible oak tree darkening with winter.
Did you find the city of isolated men beyond mountains?
Or have you been holding the end of a frayed rope
For a thousand years?

## In Fear of Harvests

It has happened
Before: nearby,
The nostrils of slow horses
Breathe evenly,
And the brown bees drag their high garlands,
Heavily,
Toward hives of snow.

## Autumn Begins in Martins Ferry, Ohio

In the Shreve High football stadium,
I think of Polacks nursing long beers in Tiltonsville,
And gray faces of Negroes in the blast furnace at Benwood,
And the ruptured night watchman of Wheeling Steel,
Dreaming of heroes.

All the proud fathers are ashamed to go home.
Their women cluck like starved pullets,
Dying for love.

Therefore,
Their sons grow suicidally beautiful
At the beginning of October,
And gallop terribly against each other's bodies.

## Lying in a Hammock at William Duffy's Farm in Pine Island, Minnesota

Over my head, I see the bronze butterfly,
Asleep on the black trunk,
Blowing like a leaf in green shadow.
Down the ravine behind the empty house,
The cowbells follow one another
Into the distances of the afternoon.
To my right,
In a field of sunlight between two pines,
The droppings of last year's horses
Blaze up into golden stones.
I lean back, as the evening darkens and comes on.
A chicken hawk floats over, looking for home.
I have wasted my life.

## The Jewel

There is this cave
In the air behind my body
That nobody is going to touch:
A cloister, a silence
Closing around a blossom of fire.
When I stand upright in the wind,
My bones turn to dark emeralds.

## Fear Is What Quickens Me

1
Many animals that our fathers killed in America
Had quick eyes.
They stared about wildly,
When the moon went dark.
The new moon falls into the freight yards
Of cities in the south,
But the loss of the moon to the dark hands of Chicago
Does not matter to the deer
In this northern field.

2
What is that tall woman doing
There, in the trees?
I can hear rabbits and mourning doves whispering together
In the dark grass, there
Under the trees.

3
I look about wildly.

## Stages on a Journey Westward

1
I began in Ohio.
I still dream of home.
Near Mansfield, enormous dobbins enter dark barns in autumn,
Where they can be lazy, where they can munch little apples,
Or sleep long.
But by night now, in the bread lines my father
Prowls, I cannot find him: So far off,
1500 miles or so away, and yet
I can hardly sleep.
In a blue rag the old man limps to my bed,
Leading a blind horse
Of gentleness.
In 1932, grimy with machinery, he sang me
A lullaby of a goosegirl.
Outside the house, the slag heaps waited.


2
In western Minnesota, just now,
I slept again.
In my dream, I crouched over a fire.
The only human beings between me and the Pacific Ocean
Were old Indians, who wanted to kill me.
They squat and stare for hours into small fires
Far off in the mountains.
The blades of their hatchets are dirty with the grease
Of huge, silent buffaloes.

3
It is dawn.
I am shivering,
Even beneath a huge eiderdown.
I came in last night, drunk,
And left the oil stove cold.
I listen a long time, now, to the flurries.
Snow howls all around me, out of the abandoned prairies.
It sounds like the voices of bums and gamblers,
Rattling through the bare nineteenth-century whorehouses
In Nevada.


4
Defeated for re-election,
The half-educated sheriff of Mukilteo, Washington,
Has been drinking again.
He leads me up the cliff, tottering.
Both drunk, we stand among the graves.
Miners paused here on the way up to Alaska.
Angry, they spaded their broken women's bodies
Into ditches of crab grass.
I lie down between tombstones.
At the bottom of the cliff
America is over and done with.
America,
Plunged into the dark furrows
Of the sea again.

## How My Fever Left

I can still hear her.
She hobbles downstairs to the kitchen.
She is swearing at the dishes.
She slaps her grease rags
Into a basket,
And slings it over her skinny forearm, crooked
With hatred, and stomps outside.
I can hear my father downstairs,
Standing without a coat in the open back door,
Calling to the old bat across the snow.
She's forgotten her black shawl,
But I see her through my window, sneering,
Flapping upward
Toward some dark church on the hill.
She has to meet somebody else, and
It's no use, she won't listen,
She's gone.

## Two Poems About President Harding

One: *His Death*

In Marion, the honey locust trees are falling.
Everybody in town remembers the white hair,
The campaign of a lost summer, the front porch
Open to the public, and the vaguely stunned smile
Of a lucky man.

"Neighbor, I want to be helpful," he said once.
Later, "You think I'm honest, don't you?"
Weeping drunk.

I am drunk this evening in 1961,
In a jag for my countryman,
Who died of crab meat on the way back from Alaska.
Everyone knows that joke.

How many honey locusts have fallen,
Pitched rootlong into the open graves of strip mines,
Since the First World War ended
And Wilson the gaunt deacon jogged sullenly
Into silence?
Tonight,
The cancerous ghosts of old con men
Shed their leaves.
For a proud man,
Lost between the turnpike near Cleveland
And the chiropractors' signs looming among dead mulberry trees,
There is no place left to go
But home.

"Warren lacks mentality," one of his friends said.

Yet he was beautiful, he was the snowfall
Turned to white stallions standing still
Under dark elm trees.

He died in public. He claimed the secret right
To be ashamed.


Two: *His Tomb in Ohio*

". . . he died of a busted gut."
    —Mencken, on Bryan

A hundred slag piles north of us,
At the mercy of the moon and rain,
He lies in his ridiculous
Tomb, our fellow citizen.
No, I have never seen that place,
Where many shadows of faceless thieves
Chuckle and stumble and embrace
On beer cans, stogie butts, and graves.

One holiday, one rainy week
After the country fell apart,
Hoover and Coolidge came to speak
And snivel about his broken heart.
His grave, a huge absurdity,
Embarrassed cops and visitors.
Hoover and Coolidge crept away
By night, and women closed their doors.

Now junkmen call their children in
Before they catch their death of cold;
Young lovers let the moon begin
Its quick spring; and the day grows old;
The mean one-legger who rakes up leaves
Has chased the loafers out of the park;
Minnegan Leonard half-believes
In God, and the poolroom goes dark;

America goes on, goes on
Laughing, and Harding was a fool.
Even his big pretentious stone
Lays him bare to ridicule.
I know it. But don't look at me.
By God, I didn't start this mess.
Whatever moon and rain may be,
The hearts of men are merciless.

# Eisenhower's Visit to Franco, 1959

"... we die of cold and not of darkness."
                                        —Unamuno

The American hero must triumph over
The forces of darkness.
He has flown through the very light of heaven
And come down in the slow dusk
Of Spain.

Franco stands in a shining circle of police.
His arms open in welcome.
He promises all dark things
Will be hunted down.

State police yawn in the prisons.
Antonio Machado follows the moon
Down a road of white dust,
To a cave of silent children
Under the Pyrenees.
Wine darkens in stone jars in villages.
Wine sleeps in the mouths of old men, it is a dark red color.

Smiles glitter in Madrid.
Eisenhower has touched hands with Franco, embracing
In a glare of photographers.
Clean new bombers from America muffle their engines
And glide down now.
Their wings shine in the searchlights
Of bare fields,
In Spain.

# Two Hangovers

*Number One*

I slouch in bed.
Beyond the streaked trees of my window,
All groves are bare.
Locusts and poplars change to unmarried women
Sorting slate from anthracite
Between railroad ties:
The yellow-bearded winter of the depression
Is still alive somewhere, an old man
Counting his collection of bottle caps
In a tarpaper shack under the cold trees
Of my grave.

I still feel half drunk,
And all those old women beyond my window
Are hunching toward the graveyard.

Drunk, mumbling Hungarian,
The sun staggers in,
And his big stupid face pitches
Into the stove.
For two hours I have been dreaming
Of green butterflies searching for diamonds
In coal seams;
And children chasing each other for a game
Through the hills of fresh graves.
But the sun has come home drunk from the sea,
And a sparrow outside
Sings of the Hanna Coal Co. and the dead moon.

The filaments of cold light bulbs tremble
In music like delicate birds.
Ah, turn it off.


*Number Two: I Try to Waken and Greet the World Once Again*

In a pine tree,
A few yards away from my window sill,
A brilliant blue jay is springing up and down, up and down,
On a branch.
I laugh, as I see him abandon himself
To entire delight, for he knows as well as I do
That the branch will not break.

## Depressed by a Book of Bad Poetry, I Walk Toward an Unused Pasture and Invite the Insects to Join Me

Relieved, I let the book fall behind a stone.
I climb a slight rise of grass.
I do not want to disturb the ants
Who are walking single file up the fence post,
Carrying small white petals,
Casting shadows so frail that I can see through them.
I close my eyes for a moment, and listen.
The old grasshoppers
Are tired, they leap heavily now,
Their thighs are burdened.
I want to hear them, they have clear sounds to make.
Then lovely, far off, a dark cricket begins
In the maple trees.

## Beginning

The moon drops one or two feathers into the field.
The dark wheat listens.
Be still.
Now.
There they are, the moon's young, trying
Their wings.
Between trees, a slender woman lifts up the lovely shadow
Of her face, and now she steps into the air, now she is gone
Wholly, into the air.
I stand alone by an elder tree, I do not dare breathe
Or move.
I listen.
The wheat leans back toward its own darkness,
And I lean toward mine.

## From a Bus Window in Central Ohio, Just Before a Thunder Shower

Cribs loaded with roughage huddle together
Before the north clouds.
The wind tiptoes between poplars.
The silver maple leaves squint
Toward the ground.
An old farmer, his scarlet face
Apologetic with whiskey, swings back a barn door
And calls a hundred black-and-white Holsteins
From the clover field.

## Trying to Pray

This time, I have left my body behind me, crying
In its dark thorns.
Still,
There are good things in this world.
It is dusk.
It is the good darkness
Of women's hands that touch loaves.
The spirit of a tree begins to move.
I touch leaves.
I close my eyes, and think of water.

## Arriving in the Country Again

The white house is silent.
My friends can't hear me yet.
The flicker who lives in the bare tree at the field's edge
Pecks once and is still for a long time.
I stand still in the late afternoon.
My face is turned away from the sun.
A horse grazes in my long shadow.

## A Prayer to Escape from the Market Place

I renounce the blindness of the magazines.
I want to lie down under a tree.
This is the only duty that is not death.
This is the everlasting happiness
Of small winds.
Suddenly,
A pheasant flutters, and I turn
Only to see him vanishing at the damp edge
Of the road.

## Today I Was Happy, So I Made This Poem

As the plump squirrel scampers
Across the roof of the corncrib,
The moon suddenly stands up in the darkness,
And I see that it is impossible to die.
Each moment of time is a mountain.
An eagle rejoices in the oak trees of heaven,
Crying
*This is what I wanted.*

# Mary Bly

I sit here, doing nothing, alone, worn out by long winter.
I feel the light breath of the newborn child.
Her face is smooth as the side of an apricot,
Eyes quick as her blond mother's hands.
She has full, soft, red hair, and as she lies quiet
In her tall mother's arms, her delicate hands
Weave back and forth.
I feel the seasons changing beneath me,
Under the floor.
She is braiding the waters of air into the plaited manes
Of happy colts.
They canter, without making a sound, along the shores
Of melting snow.

# A Blessing

Just off the highway to Rochester, Minnesota,
Twilight bounds softly forth on the grass.
And the eyes of those two Indian ponies
Darken with kindness.
They have come gladly out of the willows
To welcome my friend and me.
We step over the barbed wire into the pasture
Where they have been grazing all day, alone.
They ripple tensely, they can hardly contain their happiness
That we have come.
They bow shyly as wet swans. They love each other.
There is no loneliness like theirs.
At home once more,
They begin munching the young tufts of spring in the darkness.
I would like to hold the slenderer one in my arms,
For she has walked over to me
And nuzzled my left hand.
She is black and white,
Her mane falls wild on her forehead,
And the light breeze moves me to caress her long ear
That is delicate as the skin over a girl's wrist.
Suddenly I realize
That if I stepped out of my body I would break
Into blossom.

## Milkweed

While I stood here, in the open, lost in myself,
I must have looked a long time
Down the corn rows, beyond grass,
The small house,
White walls, animals lumbering toward the barn.
I look down now. It is all changed.
Whatever it was I lost, whatever I wept for
Was a wild, gentle thing, the small dark eyes
Loving me in secret.
It is here. At a touch of my hand,
The air fills with delicate creatures
From the other world.

# A Dream of Burial

Nothing was left of me
But my right foot
And my left shoulder.
They lay white as the skein of a spider floating
In a field of snow toward a dark building
Tilted and stained by wind.
Inside the dream, I dreamed on.

A parade of old women
Sang softly above me,
Faint mosquitoes near still water.

So I waited, in my corridor.
I listened for the sea
To call me.
I knew that, somewhere outside, the horse
Stood saddled, browsing in grass,
Waiting for me.

from

# Shall We Gather at the River

# The Minneapolis Poem

*to John Logan*

1

I wonder how many old men last winter
Hungry and frightened by namelessness prowled
The Mississippi shore
Lashed blind by the wind, dreaming
Of suicide in the river.
The police remove their cadavers by daybreak
And turn them in somewhere.
Where?
How does the city keep lists of its fathers
Who have no names?
By Nicollet Island I gaze down at the dark water
So beautifully slow.
And I wish my brothers good luck
And a warm grave.


2

The Chippewa young men
Stab one another shrieking
Jesus Christ.
Split-lipped homosexuals limp in terror of assault.
High school backfields search under benches
Near the Post Office. Their faces are the rich
Raw bacon without eyes.
The Walker Art Center crowd stare
At one another
And the Guthrie Theater crowd stare
At the Guthrie Theater.

3

Tall Negro girls from Chicago
Listen to light songs.
They know when the supposed patron
Is a plainclothesman.
A cop's palm
Is a roach dangling down the scorched fangs
Of a light bulb.
The soul of a cop's eyes
Is an eternity of Sunday daybreak in the suburbs
Of Juárez, Mexico.


4

The legless beggars are gone, carried away
By white birds.
The Artificial Limbs Exchange is gutted
And sown with lime.
The whalebone crutches and hand-me-down trusses
Huddle together dreaming in a desolation
Of dry groins.
I think of poor men astonished to waken
Exposed in broad daylight by the blade
Of a strange plough.


5

All over the walls of comb cells
Automobiles perfumed and blindered
Consent with a mutter of high good humor
To take their two naps a day.
Without sound windows glide back
Into dusk.

The sockets of a thousand blind bee graves tier upon tier
Tower not quite toppling.
There are men in this city who labor dawn after dawn
To sell me my death.


6

But I could not bear
To allow my poor brother my body to die
In Minneapolis.
The old man Walt Whitman our countryman
Is now in America our country
Dead.
But he was not buried in Minneapolis
At least.
And no more may I be
Please God.


7

I want to be lifted up
By some great white bird unknown to the police,
And soar for a thousand miles and be carefully hidden
Modest and golden as one last corn grain,
Stored with the secrets of the wheat and the mysterious lives
Of the unnamed poor.

## Inscription for the Tank

My life was never so precious
To me as now.
I gape unbelieving at those two lines
Of my words, caught and frisked naked.

If they loomed secret and dim
On the wall of the drunk-tank,
Scraped there by a raw fingernail
In the trickling crusts of gray mold,

Surely the plainest thug who read them
Would cluck with the ancient pity.
Men have a right to thank God for their loneliness.
The walls are hysterical with their dank messages.

But the last hophead is gone
With the quick of his name
Bleeding away down a new wall
Blank as his nails.

I wish I had walked outside
To wade in the sea, drowsing and soothed;
I wish I had copied some words from Isaiah,
Kabir, Ansari, oh Whitman, oh anyone, anyone.

But I wrote down mine, and now
I must read them forever, even
When the wings in my shoulders cringe up
At the cold's fangs, as now.

Of all my lives, the one most secret to me,
Folded deep in a book never written,
Locked up in a dream of a still place,
I have blurted out.

I have heard weeping in secret
And quick nails broken.
Let the dead pray for their own dead.
What is their pity to me?

## Before a Cashier's Window in a Department Store

1

The beautiful cashier's white face has risen once more
Behind a young manager's shoulder.
They whisper together, and stare
Straight into my face.
I feel like grabbing a stray child
Or a skinny old woman
And diving into a cellar, crouching
Under a stone bridge, praying myself sick,
Till the troops pass.


2

Why should he care? He goes.
I slump deeper.
In my frayed coat, I am pinned down
By debt. He nods,
Commending my flesh to the pity of the daws of God.


3

Am I dead? And, if not, why not?
For she sails there, alone, looming in the heaven of the beautiful.
She knows
The bulldozers will scrape me up
After dark, behind
The officers' club.

Beneath her terrible blaze, my skeleton
Glitters out. I am the dark. I am the dark
Bone I was born to be.


4
Tu Fu woke shuddering on a battlefield
Once, in the dead of night, and made out
The mangled women, sorting
The haggard slant-eyes.
The moon was up.


5
I am hungry. In two more days
It will be spring. So this
Is what it feels like.

## Speak

To speak in a flat voice
Is all that I can do.
I have gone every place
Asking for you.
Wondering where to turn
And how the search would end
And the last streetlight spin
Above me blind.

Then I returned rebuffed
And saw under the sun
The race not to the swift
Nor the battle won.
Liston dives in the tank,
Lord, in Lewiston, Maine,
And Ernie Doty's drunk
In hell again.

And Jenny, oh my Jenny
Whom I love, rhyme be damned,
Has broken her spare beauty
In a whorehouse old.
She left her new baby
In a bus-station can,
And sprightly danced away
Through Jacksontown.

Which is a place I know,
One where I got picked up
A few shrunk years ago
By a good cop.
Believe it, Lord, or not.
Don't ask me who he was.
I speak of flat defeat
In a flat voice.

I have gone forward with
Some, a few lonely some.
They have fallen to death.
I die with them.
Lord, I have loved Thy cursed,
The beauty of Thy house:
Come down. Come down. Why dost
Thou hide Thy face?

## Outside Fargo, North Dakota

Along the sprawled body of the derailed Great Northern freight car,
I strike a match slowly and lift it slowly.
No wind.

Beyond town, three heavy white horses
Wade all the way to their shoulders
In a silo shadow.

Suddenly the freight car lurches.
The door slams back, a man with a flashlight
Calls me good evening.
I nod as I write down good evening, lonely
And sick for home.

## Living by the Red River

Blood flows in me, but what does it have to do
With the rain that is falling?
In me, scarlet-jacketed armies march into the rain
Across dark fields. My blood lies still,
Indifferent to cannons on the ships of imperialists
Drifting offshore.
Sometimes I have to sleep
In dangerous places, on cliffs underground,
Walls that still hold the whole prints
Of ancient ferns.

## To Flood Stage Again

In Fargo, North Dakota, a man
Warned me the river might rise
To flood stage again.
On the bridge, a girl hurries past me, alone,
Unhappy face.
Will she pause in wet grass somewhere?
Behind my eyes she stands tiptoe, yearning for confused sparrows
To fetch a bit of string and dried wheatbeard
To line her outstretched hand.
I open my eyes and gaze down
At the dark water.

## Youth

Strange bird,
His song remains secret.
He worked too hard to read books.
He never heard how Sherwood Anderson
Got out of it, and fled to Chicago, furious to free himself
From his hatred of factories.
My father toiled fifty years
At Hazel-Atlas Glass,
Caught among girders that smash the kneecaps
Of dumb honyaks.
Did he shudder with hatred in the cold shadow of grease?
Maybe. But my brother and I do know
He came home as quiet as the evening.

He will be getting dark, soon,
And loom through new snow.
I know his ghost will drift home
To the Ohio River, and sit down, alone,
Whittling a root.
He will say nothing.
The waters flow past, older, younger
Than he is, or I am.

## The Life

Murdered, I went, risen,
Where the murderers are,
That black ditch
Of river.

And if I come back to my only country
With a white rose on my shoulder,
What is that to you?
It is the grave
In blossom.

It is the trillium of darkness,
It is hell, it is the beginning of winter,
It is a ghost town of Etruscans who have no names
Any more.

It is the old loneliness.
It is.
And it is
The last time.

## The Lights in the Hallway

The lights in the hallway
Have been out a long time.
I clasp her,
Terrified by the roundness of the earth
And its apples and the voluptuous rings
Of poplar trees, the secret Africas,
The children they give us.
She is slim enough.
Her knee feels like the face
Of a surprised lioness
Nursing the lost children
Of a gazelle by pure accident.
In that body I long for,
The Gabon poets gaze for hours
Between boughs toward heaven, their noble faces
Too secret to weep.
How do I know what color her hair is? I float among
Lonely animals, longing
For the red spider who is God.

## In Memory of Leopardi

I have gone past all those times when the poets
Were beautiful as only
The rich can be. The cold bangles
Of the moon grazed one of my shoulders,
And so to this day,
And beyond, I carry
The sliver of a white city, the barb of a jewel
In my left clavicle that hunches.
Tonight I sling
A scrambling sack of oblivions and lame prayers
On my right good arm. The Ohio River
Has flown by me twice, the dark jubilating
Isaiah of mill and smoke marrow. Blind son
Of a meadow of huge horses, lover of drowned islands
Above Steubenville, blind father
Of my halt gray wing:
Now I limp on, knowing
The moon strides behind me, swinging
The scimitar of the divinity that struck down
The hunchback in agony
When he saw her, naked, carrying away his last sheep
Through the Asian rocks.

# Two Postures Beside a Fire

1
Tonight I watch my father's hair,
As he sits dreaming near his stove.
Knowing my feather of despair,
He sent me an owl's plume for love,
Lest I not know, so I've come home.
Tonight Ohio, where I once
Hounded and cursed my loneliness,
Shows me my father, who broke stones,
Wrestled and mastered great machines,
And rests, shadowing his lovely face.


2
Nobly his hands fold together in his repose.
He is proud of me, believing
I have done strong things among men and become a man
Of place among men of place in the large cities.
I will not waken him.
I have come home alone, without wife or child
To delight him. Awake, solitary and welcome,
I too sit near his stove, the lines
Of an ugly age scarring my face, and my hands
Twitch nervously about.

# For the Marsh's Birthday

As a father to his son, as a friend to his friend,
Be pleased to show mercy, O God.


I was alone once, waiting
For you, what you might be.
I heard your grass birds, fluting
Down a long road, to me.
Wholly for you, for you,
I was lonely, lonely.

For how was I to know
Your voice, or understand
The Irish cockatoo?
Never on sea or land
Had I heard a voice that was
Greener than grass.

Oh the voice lovelier was
Than a crow's dreaming face,
His secret face, that smiles
Alive in a dead place.
Oh I was lonely, lonely:
What were the not to me?

The not were nothing then.
Now, let the not become
Nothing, and so remain,
Till the bright grass birds come
Home to the singing tree.
Then, let them be.

Let them be living, then,
They have been dead so long.
Love, I am sick of pain
And sick with my longing,
My Irish cockatoo,
To listen to you,

Now you are all alive
And not a dream at all;
Now there are more than five
Voices I listen to
Call, call, call, call, call, call:
My Irish cockatoo.

## Lifting Illegal Nets by Flashlight

The carp are secrets
Of the creation: I do not
Know if they are lonely.
The poachers drift with an almost frightening
Care under the bridge.
Water is a luminous
Mirror of swallows' nests. The stars
Have gone down.
What does my anguish
Matter? Something
The color
Of a puma has plunged through this net, and is gone.
This is the firmest
Net I ever saw, and yet something
Is gone lonely
Into the headwaters of the Minnesota.

## In Response to a Rumor That the Oldest Whorehouse in Wheeling, West Virginia, Has Been Condemned

I will grieve alone,
As I strolled alone, years ago, down along
The Ohio shore.
I hid in the hobo jungle weeds
Upstream from the sewer main,
Pondering, gazing.

I saw, down river,
At Twenty-third and Water Streets
By the vinegar works,
The doors open in early evening.
Swinging their purses, the women
Poured down the long street to the river
And into the river.

I do not know how it was
They could drown every evening.
What time near dawn did they climb up the other shore,
Drying their wings?

For the river at Wheeling, West Virginia,
Has only two shores:
The one in hell, the other
In Bridgeport, Ohio.

And nobody would commit suicide, only
To find beyond death
Bridgeport, Ohio.

## To the Muse

It is all right. All they do
Is go in by dividing
One rib from another. I wouldn't
Lie to you. It hurts
Like nothing I know. All they do
Is burn their way in with a wire.
It forks in and out a little like the tongue
Of that frightened garter snake we caught
At Cloverfield, you and me, Jenny
So long ago.

I would lie to you
If I could.
But the only way I can get you to come up
Out of the suckhole, the south face
Of the Powhatan pit, is to tell you
What you know:

You come up after dark, you poise alone
With me on the shore.
I lead you back to this world.

Three lady doctors in Wheeling open
Their offices at night.
I don't have to call them, they are always there.
But they only have to put the knife once
Under your breast.
Then they hang their contraption.
And you bear it.

It's awkward a while. Still, it lets you
Walk about on tiptoe if you don't
Jiggle the needle.
It might stab your heart, you see.
The blade hangs in your lung and the tube
Keeps it draining.
That way they only have to stab you
Once. Oh Jenny,
I wish to God I had made this world, this scurvy
And disastrous place. I
Didn't, I can't bear it
Either, I don't blame you, sleeping down there
Face down in the unbelievable silk of spring,
Muse of black sand,
Alone.

I don't blame you, I know
The place where you lie.
I admit everything. But look at me.
How can I live without you?
Come up to me, love,
Out of the river, or I will
Come down to you.

from

# New Poems (*in* Collected Poems)

## Small Frogs Killed on the Highway

Still,
I would leap too
Into the light,
If I had the chance.
It is everything, the wet green stalk of the field
On the other side of the road.
They crouch there, too, faltering in terror
And take strange wing. Many
Of the dead never moved, but many
Of the dead are alive forever in the split second
Auto headlights more sudden
Than their drivers know.
The drivers burrow backward into dank pools
Where nothing begets
Nothing.

Across the road, tadpoles are dancing
On the quarter thumbnail
Of the moon. They can't see,
Not yet.

## Northern Pike

All right. Try this,
Then. Every body
I know and care for,
And every body
Else is going
To die in a loneliness
I can't imagine and a pain
I don't know. We had
To go on living. We
Untangled the net, we slit
The body of this fish
Open from the hinge of the tail
To a place beneath the chin
I wish I could sing of.
I would just as soon we let
The living go on living.
An old poet whom we believe in
Said the same thing, and so
We paused among the dark cattails and prayed
For the muskrats,
For the ripples below their tails,
For the little movements that we knew the crawdads were making
      under water,
For the right-hand wrist of my cousin who is a policeman.
We prayed for the game warden's blindness.
We prayed for the road home.
We ate the fish.
There must be something very beautiful in my body,
I am so happy.

from

# Two Citizens

# The Old WPA Swimming Pool in Martins Ferry, Ohio

I am almost afraid to write down
This thing. I must have been,
Say, seven years old. That afternoon,
The families of the WPA had come out
To have a good time celebrating
A long gouge in the ground,
That the fierce husbands
Had filled with concrete.

We knew even then the Ohio
River was dying.
Most of the good men who lived along that shore
Wanted to be in love and give good love
To beautiful women, who weren't pretty,
And to small children like me who wondered,
What the hell is this?

When people don't have quite enough to eat
In August, and the river,
That is supposed to be some holiness,
Starts dying,

They swim in the earth. Uncle Sherman,
Uncle Willie, Uncle Emerson, and my father
Helped dig that hole in the ground.

I had seen by that time two or three
Holes in the ground,
And you know what they were.

But this one was not the usual, cheap
Economics, it was not the solitary
Scar on a poor man's face, that respectable
Hole in the ground you used to be able to buy
After you died for seventy-five dollars and
Your wages tached for six months by the Heslop
Brothers.

Brothers, dear God.

No, this hole was filled with water,
And suddenly I flung myself into the water.
All I had on was a jockstrap my brother stole
From a miserable football team.

Oh never mind, Jesus Christ, my father
And my uncles dug a hole in the ground,
No grave for once. It is going to be hard
For you to believe: when I rose from that water,

A little girl who belonged to somebody else,
A face thin and haunted appeared
Over my left shoulder, and whispered, Take care now,
Be patient, and live.

I have loved you all this time,
And didn't even know
I am alive.

## The Art of the Fugue: A Prayer

Radiant silence in Fiesole
And the long climb up a hill which is only one feather
Of the sky, and to set out within the sky,
As the dark happy Florentine would surely gather
All that he had to gather and every night set forth
And enter the pearl.

Florence below our hands, the city that yielded
Up the last secret of Hell.
Fiesole below me and around me and the wings
Of the invisible musician Brother Esposito folded
Around me and my girl.

And the organ
Silent in its longing for the only love.
And Bach and Dante meeting and praying
Before the music began.

And a little bell ringing halfway down the hill.

And me there a long way from the cold dream of Hell.
Me, there, alone, at last,
At last with the dust of my dust,
As far away as I will ever get from dying,
And the two great poets of God in the silence
Meeting together.

And Esposito the organist waiting to begin.
And the little bell halfway down delicately drifting off.

And Florence down there darkening, waiting to begin.

And me there alone at last with my only love,
Waiting to begin.

Whoever you are, ambling past my grave,
My name worn thin as the shawl of the lovely hill town
Fiesole, the radiance and silence of the sky,
Listen to me:

Though love can be scarcely imaginable Hell,
By God, it is not a lie.

## To the Creature of the Creation

Lonely as my desire is,
I have no daughter.
I will not die by fire, I
Shall die by water.

Water is fire, the wand
Some body wandering near,
Limping to understand,
If only he somewhere

Could find that lonely thing
That fears him, yet comes out
To look through him and sing.

He cannot do without.

Without the moon, and me.
And who is she?
This poem frightens me
So secretly, so much,
It makes me hard to touch
Your body's secret places.
We are each other's faces.

No, I ain't much.
The only tongue I can write in
Is my Ohioan.
There, most people are poor.

I thought I could not stand it
To go home any more,
Yet I go home, every year,
To calm down my wild mother,
And talk long with my brother.

What have I got to do?
The sky is shattering,
The plain sky grows so blue.
Some day I have to die,
As everyone must do
Alone, alone, alone,
Peaceful as peaceful stone.
You are the earth's body.
I will die on the wing.
To me, you are everything
That matters, chickadee.
You live so much in me.
Chickadees sing in the snow.
I will die on the wing,
I love you so.

from

**Selected Prose Pieces** (*in* Above the River)

# The Gift of Change

Of all the creatures, they seem to know best the art of sunning themselves. Without brooding unhappily, they understand where the best shades are. It is next to impossible to catch them and imprison them in the usual human ways, because they live in perpetual surrender: They love to become whatever it is that gazes upon them or holds them. They can turn as precisely green as the faintest hint of moss-shadow thirty seconds after noon, or a little gray knitted into silver of drying algae buoyed up ashore and abandoned there to the random wind of children's feet in flight.

But the lizard lying beside me now has gone too far. Wholly abandoning himself to his gift of change, he lifts his head above the edge of a linden blossom freshly fallen and alone. His exquisite hands have given up clinging to anything. They lie open. The leaf on the flower is so smooth, a light wind could blow him away. I wonder if he knows. If he knows, I wonder that my breath doesn't blow him away. I am that close to him, and he that close to me. He has gone too far into the world to turn back now. His tail has become a spot on the sun, the delicate crease between his shoulder blades, the fold in a linden leaf, his tongue finer and purer than a wild hair in my nostril, his hands opener than my hands. It is too late to turn back into himself. I can't even faintly begin to understand what is happening behind his serene face, but to me he looks like the happiest creature alive in Italy.

# A Snail at Assisi

The snail shell has lain up here all summer along, I suppose. It is smaller than my thumbnail, where it rests now, but it casts its light shadow huge on the ground, and my shadow is there, following very carefully. Already the light has taken my shadow into the air and laid it down the slope below me, where it grows longer and longer, always moving, yet hardly to be seen moving. The air is dry far up here on the highest hill in Assisi, on the far side of the fortress wall where the earth falls nearly straight down. Even as I squint in the sun and try to bear it alive, I wonder how the tiny snail was alive and climbed and climbed and made it all the way up to this pinnacle, the armed building and the arrow-skewered wall. The great hollow skeleton of this fortress is empty now, its back turned away from Francis's solitary hill, its face still set grimly toward Perugia. The snail is long gone, maybe lifted high into sunlight, devoured by song-birds between one fortress and another. By this time, one more long summer afternoon is nearly over. My shadow and the shadow of the snail shell are one and the same.

## The Lambs on the Boulder

I hear that the Comune di Padova has an exhibition of master-pieces from Giotto to Mantegna. Giotto is the master of angels, and Mantegna is the master of the dead Christ, one of the few human beings who seems to have understood that Christ did indeed come down from the cross after all, in response to the famous jeering invitation, and that the Christ who came down was a cadaver. Mantegna's dead Christ looks exactly like a skidroad bum fished by the cops out of the Mississippi in autumn just before daylight and hurried off in a tarpaulin-shrouded garbage truck and deposited in another tangle of suicides and befuddled drunkards at the rear entrance to the University of Minnesota medical school. Eternity is a vast space of distances as well as a curving infinity of time.

No doubt the exhibition in noble Padova will be a glory to behold.

But there is a littler glory that I love best. It is a story, which so intensely ought to be real that it is real.

One afternoon the mature medieval master Cimabue was taking a walk in the countryside and paused in the shade to watch a shepherd boy. The child was trying to scratch sketches of his lambs on a boulder at the edge of the field. He used nothing, for he could find nothing, but a little sharp pebble.

Cimabue took the shepherd boy home with him and gave him some parchment and a nail or a crayon or something or other, and began to show him how to draw and form lines into the grandeur of faces other than the sweet faces of sheep.

The shepherd boy was Giotto, and he learned how to draw and form lines into the grandeur of faces other than the sweet faces of sheep. I don't give a damn whether you believe this story or not.

I do. I have seen faces of angels drawn by Giotto. If angels do not look like Giotto's angels, they have been neglecting their health behind God's back.

One of my idle wishes is to find that field where Cimabue stood in the shade and watched the boy Giotto scratching his stone with his pebble.

I would not be so foolish as to prefer the faces of the boy's lambs to the faces of his angels. One has to act his age sooner or later.

Still, this little planet of rocks and grass is all we have to start with. How pretty it would be, the sweet faces of the boy Giotto's lambs gouged, with infinite and still uncertain and painful care, on the side of a boulder at the edge of a country field.

I wonder how long Cimabue stood watching before he said anything. I'll bet he watched for a very long time. He was Cimabue.

I wonder how long Giotto worked before he noticed that he was being watched. I'll bet he worked a very long time. He was Giotto.

He probably paused every so often to take a drink of water and tend to the needs of his sheep, and then returned patiently to his patient boulder, before he heard over his shoulder in the twilight the courtesy of the Italian good evening from the countryside man who stood, certainly out of the little daylight left to the shepherd and his sheep alike.

I wonder where that boulder is. I wonder if the sweet faces of the lambs are still scratched on its sunlit side.

By God I know this much. Worse men than Giotto have lived longer than Giotto lived.

And uglier things than Giotto's wobbly scratches on a coarse boulder at the edge of a grassy field are rotting and toppling into decay at this very moment. By the time I reach Padova at fifteen minutes past four this afternoon, I wouldn't be a bit surprised to hear that Rockefeller's Mall in Albany, New York, had begun to sag and ooze its grandiose slime all over the surrounding city of the plain, and it will stink in the nostrils of God Almighty like the incense burned and offered up as a putrid gift on the altars of the Lord, while the King Jeroboam the Second imprisoned the righteous for silver and sold the poor for the buckles on a pair of shoes.

Giotto's boyish hand scratched the sweet faces of lambs on a coarse stone.

I wonder where the stone is. I will never live to see it.

I lived to see the Mall in Albany, though.

In one of the mature Giotto's greatest glories, a huge choir of his unutterably beautiful angels are lifting their faces and are becoming the sons of the morning, singing out of pure happiness the praises of God.

Far back in the angelic choir, a slightly smaller angel has folded his wings. He has turned slightly away from the light and lifted his hands. You cannot even see his face. I don't know why he is weeping. But I love him best.

I think he must be wondering how long it will take Giotto to remember him, give him a drink of water, and take him back home to the fold before it gets dark and shepherd and sheep alike lose their way in the darkness of the countryside.

*Padua*

# To a Blossoming Pear Tree

# Redwings

It turns out
You can kill them.
It turns out
You can make the earth absolutely clean.

My nephew has given my younger brother
A scientific report while they both flew
In my older brother's small airplane
Over the Kokosing River, that looks

Secret, it looks like the open
Scar turning gray on the small
Of your spine.

Can you hear me?

It was only in the evening I saw a few redwings
Come out and dip their brilliant yellow
Bills in their scarlet shoulders.
Ohio was already going to hell.
But sometimes they would sit down on the creosote
Soaked pasture fence posts.
They used to be few, they used to be willowy and thin.

One afternoon, along the Ohio, where the sewer
Poured out, I found a nest,
The way they build their nests in the reeds,
So beautiful,
Redwings and solitaries.

The skinny girl I fell in love with down home
In late autumn married
A strip miner in late autumn.
Her five children are still alive,
Floating near the river.

Somebody is on the wing, somebody
Is wondering right at this moment
How to get rid of us, while we sleep.

Together among the dead gorges
Of highway construction, we flare
Across highways and drive
Motorists crazy, we fly
Down home to the river.

There, one summer evening, a dirty man
Gave me a nickel and a potato
And fell asleep by a fire.

## One Last Look at the Adige: Verona in the Rain

Some crumbling of igneous
Far off in the coverts
Of my orplidean country,
Where tall men
Are faintly bearded
Pines, now, the slow stalagmon
Gathers downward
Stone, milk of mineral
Below my graying face.
This is another river
I can still see flow by.

The Ohio must have looked
Something like this
To the people who loved it
Long before I was born.
They called the three
Slim islands of willow and poplar
Above Steubenville,
They, they, they
Called
The three slim islands
Our Sisters.

Steubenville is a black crust, America is
A shallow hell where evil
Is an easy joke, forgotten
In a week.

Oh, stay with me a little longer in the rain,
Adige.

Now, Adige, flow on.
Adige, river on earth,
Only you can hear
A half-witted angel drawling Ohioan
In the warm Italian rain.

In the middle of my own life
I woke up and found myself
Dying, fair enough, still
Alive in the friendly city
Of my body, my secret Verona,
Milky and green,
My moving jewel, the last
Pure vein left to me.

The unrighteous heathen,
Valerio Catullo,
Was born in Verona,
And you held him in the curve of your arm.
He couldn't stand it.
He left home and went straight
To hell in Rome.
*Io factum male io miselle*
*Adige*, the lights
Have gone out on the stone bridge,
Where I stand, alone,
A dark city on one shore,
And, on the other,
A dark forest.

# The Wheeling Gospel Tabernacle

Homer Rhodeheaver, who was the evangelist Billy Sunday's psalmodist and shill at the offertory, did something in the year of Our Lord 1925 that made both of my parents almost ecstatic with happiness all the rest of their lives, until they died within a few months of each other in 1973.

Just as the Reverend Doctor Sunday was admonishing the congregation in congress assembled with his customary warning that they warn't no virtue in the clinking of shekels, a wicked sound; just as the Reverend Doctor was in full oratorical blossoming cry in praise of each silken soft certain rustle of one twenty-dollar bill against another in the wicker collection plate; just as the former semi-professional baseball player of the Lord God Almighty Lord of Hosts was advising how as "Bruthern, a twenty don't take up no more room in that there plate than a wun"—it happened.

One of Doctor Sunday's locally hired ushers glided to the minister's side and with ghostly discretion reported to the evangelical ear that the cops from Pittsburgh had just left Weirton, West Virginia, and were hurtling down the West Virginia Route 40 in their Prohibition-style armored Cord cars, bound to catch Homer Rhodeheaver in full song. He was wanted in Pittsburgh on a paternity charge.

By the time the Pittsburgh cops burst into the Wheeling Gospel Tabernacle, it was as empty and dark as the waiting room of a speakeasy. Where had the brethren gone? Some thought that Doctor Sunday ascended. I lean toward the opinion that the two laborers in the vineyards of the Lord skinned the populace of Benwood down the river the next day, and that possibly Homer had time between hymns to make some lonely widow happy.

The year was 1925. My mother and father got one of their chances to laugh like hell for the sheer joy of laughter before the Great Depression began.

They were younger than I am this year. I was born two years after Homer Rhodeheaver and Billy Sunday appeared to run up their crusading flag near the blast furnace down the Ohio River for what was surely a one-night stand.

For all I know, my mother and father loved each other in 1925. For all I know, Homer Rhodeheaver is still in full flight from the Paternity Squad of the Pittsburgh Police Department. For all I know, Homer Rhodeheaver really was a glorious singer of the great hymns down home. For all I know, he carried a better tune than he knew. Women heard him in Pittsburgh. Maybe women heard him in the Wheeling Gospel Tabernacle. Maybe Jehovah was drowsing, and Eros heard the prayer and figured that love after all was love, no matter what language a man sang it in, so what the hell.

Little I know. I can pitch a pretty fair tune myself, for all I know.

# The Flying Eagles of Troop 62

Ralph Neal was the Scoutmaster. He was still a young man. He liked us.

I have no doubt he knew perfectly well we were each of us masturbating unhappily in secret caves and shores.

The soul of patience, he waited while we smirked behind each other's backs, mocking and parodying the Scout Law, trying to imitate the oratorical rotundities of Winston Churchill in a Southern Ohio accent:

"Ay scout is trusswortha, loll, hailpful, frenly, curtchuss, kand, abaydent, chairful, thrifta, dapraved, clane, and letcherass."

Ralph Neal knew all about the pain of the aching stones in our twelve-year-old groins, the lava swollen halfway between our peckers and our nuts that were still green and sour as half-ripe apples two full months before the football season began.

Socrates loved his friend the traitor Alcibiades for his beauty and for what he might become.

I think Ralph Neal loved us for our scrawniness, our acne, our fear; but mostly for his knowledge of what would probably become of us. He was not a fool. He knew he would never himself get out of that slime hole of a river valley, and maybe he didn't want to. The Vedantas illustrate the most sublime of ethical ideals by describing a saint who, having endured through a thousand lives every half-assed mistake and unendurable suffering possible to humanity from birth to death, refused at the last moment to enter Nirvana because he realized that his scruffy dog, suppurating at the nostrils and half mad with rabies, could not accompany him into perfect peace.

Some of us wanted to get out, and some of us wanted to and didn't.

The last I heard, Dickey Beck, a three-time loser at house-breaking, was doing life at the State Pen in Columbus.

The last I heard, Dale Headley was driving one of those milk trucks where the driver has to stand up all day and rattle his spine over the jagged street-bricks.

The last I heard from my brother-in-law, Hub Snodgrass was still dragging himself home every evening down by the river to shine, shower, shave, and spend a good hour still trying to scrape the Laughlin steel dust out of his pale skin. He never tanned much, he just burned or stayed out of the river.

The last I heard, Mike Kottelos was making book in Wheeling.

I have never gone back there down home to see Ralph Neal. My portrait hangs on one of the walls of the Martins Ferry Public Library. Ralph Neal would think I've become something. And no doubt I have, though I don't know just what. Scribbling my name in books. Christ have mercy on me alive; and after I'm dead, as Pietro Aretino of Florence requested of the priest after he had received extreme unction on his deathbed, "Now that I've been oiled, keep me from the rats."

When I think of Ralph Neal's name, I feel some kind of ice breaking open in me. I feel a garfish escaping into a hill spring where the crawdads burrow down to the pure bottom in hot weather to get the cool. I feel a rush of long fondness for that good man Ralph Neal, that good man who knew us dreadful and utterly vulnerable little bastards better than we knew ourselves, who took care of us better than we took care of ourselves, and who loved us, I reckon, because he knew damned well what would become of most of us, and it sure did, and he knew it, and he loved us anyway. The very name of America often makes me sick, and yet Ralph Neal was an American. The country is enough to drive you crazy.

# With the Shell of a Hermit Crab

*Lugete, O Veneres Cupidinesque*
      —Catullus


This lovely little life whose toes
Touched the white sand from side to side,
How delicately no one knows,
Crept from his loneliness, and died.

From deep waters long miles away
He wandered, looking for his name,
And all he found was you and me,
A quick life and a candle flame.

Today, you happen to be gone.
I sit here in the raging hell,
The city of the dead, alone,
Holding a little empty shell.

I peer into his tiny face.
It looms too huge for me to bear.
Two blocks away the sea gives place
To river. Both are everywhere.

I reach out and flick out the light.
Darkly I touch his fragile scars,
So far away, so delicate,
Stars in a wilderness of stars.

## The Silent Angel

As I sat down by the bus window in the gate of Verona, I looked over my left shoulder. A man was standing in one of the pink marble arches at the base of the great Roman Arena. He smiled at me, a gesture of the utmost sweetness, such as a human face can rarely manage to shine with, even a beloved face that loves you in return.

He seemed dressed like a musician, as well he might have been, emerging for a moment into the sunlight from one of the secluded and cool rehearsal chambers of the upper tiers of the Arena.

As the bus driver powered his motor and drew us slowly around the great public square, the Piazza Bra, the man in the half-golden rose shadow of the Arena kept his gaze on my face. He waved goodbye to me, his knowing eyes never leaving me as long as he could still see any of me at all, though how long that was I don't precisely know.

He raised his hand at the last moment to wave me out of Verona as kindly as he could. He held in his right hand what seemed to be a baton, and it hung suspended for a long instant in the vast petals of rose shadows cast down by the marble walls. Even after he had vanished back into the archway I could still see his baton.

Oh, I know it was not a baton. I was far away now, and all I could see behind me were the diminishing cicadas, lindens, and slim cedars rising, one feather folding upwards into another, into the spaces of evergreen and gold beyond the Roman Arena, beyond the river and the hills beyond the river, the beginning of everlasting change, Saint Martin's summer. All those trees, the durable and the momentary confused with one another into the eternity of Saint Augustine's despair of time. They will still be rising there long after even the Giusti Gardens, where Goethe walked, have run back to weeds, a few of my beloved lizards left to make company with them perhaps, a spider or two still designing for days and then patiently building the most delicate of ruins.

I could not afford to let myself think of the River Adige any longer, because I loved it too much. The wings of the smiling musician are folded. His baton, grown cool again by this time, rests on his knees. I can imagine that all the other musicians have risen into the riverside hills for the night, and my musician, who meant me no harm and only wanted to wave me away as gently as possible out of the beautiful space he guarded, is himself asleep with the late crickets along the river.

I turned at last away from the city, gritted my teeth, two of which are broken and snaggled, fingered the shred of pink marble in my jacket pocket, and forced my face toward Milano with its factories, London with its fear and hopelessness, and beyond that, the final place, New York, America, hell on earth.

I felt fallen. But not very happy. Nor lucky either.

The musician had not played me a single tune, he had not sung me a single song. He just waved me as gently as he could on the way out, the way that is my own, the lost way.

I suppose I asked for it. And he did his best, I suppose. He owns that heavenly city no more than I do. He may be fallen, as I am. But from a greater height, unless I miss my guess.

*Verona*

## The First Days

Optima dies prima fugit

The first thing I saw in the morning
Was a huge golden bee ploughing
His burly right shoulder into the belly
Of a sleek yellow pear
Low on a bough.
Before he could find that sudden black honey
That squirms around in there
Inside the seed, the tree could not bear any more.
The pear fell to the ground,
With the bee still half alive
Inside its body.
He would have died if I hadn't knelt down
And sliced the pear gently
A little more open.
The bee shuddered, and returned.
Maybe I should have left him alone there,
Drowning in his own delight.
The best days are the first
To flee, sang the lovely
Musician born in this town
So like my own.
I let the bee go
Among the gasworks at the edge of Mantua.

# The Fruits of the Season

It is a fresh morning of late August in Padua. After the night's rain, the sun is emerging just enough so far to begin warming the grapes, melons, peaches, nectarines, and the other fruits that will soon fill this vast square. Women and children in bright flower-print dresses are already beginning to amble from stall to stall.

At the very far end of the square I can see the azure and golden face of the town clock on the Torre dell'Orologio.

A baker with white flour sprinkled all over his boots just drifted across the extreme right corner of my eye.

It is all commonplace, ordinary, the firm shaping of the morning in an Italian city of middling size.

And yet—to my left I can see the entire front length of the Palazzo della Ragione, on whose second floor the community has arranged a huge exhibit of paintings, the enduring fruits of five hundred years.

And spread below the faces of those peculiarly tender and fierce angels, the men and women and their children are still arriving from the countryside, arranging for our slow ambling choice the heaps of grapes, melons, peaches, nectarines, and all the other fruits of the season in a glory that will not last too long.

But they will last long enough. I would rather live my life than not live it. The grapes in a smallish stall are as huge and purple as smoke. I have just eaten one. I have eaten the first fruit of the season, and I am in love.

*Padua*

# Hook

I was only a young man
In those days. On that evening
The cold was so God damned
Bitter there was nothing.
Nothing. I was in trouble
With a woman, and there was nothing
There but me and dead snow.

I stood on the street corner
In Minneapolis, lashed
This way and that.
Wind rose from some pit,
Hunting me.
Another bus to Saint Paul
Would arrive in three hours,
If I was lucky.

Then the young Sioux
Loomed beside me, his scars
Were just my age.

Ain't got no bus here
A long time, he said.
You got enough money
To get home on?

What did they do
To your hand? I answered.
He raised up his hook into the terrible starlight
And slashed the wind.

Oh, that? he said.
I had a bad time with a woman. Here,
You take this.

Did you ever feel a man hold
Sixty-five cents
In a hook,
And place it
Gently
In your freezing hand?

I took it.
It wasn't the money I needed.
But I took it.

## Beautiful Ohio

Those old Winnebago men
Knew what they were singing.
All summer long and all alone,
I had found a way
To sit on a railroad tie
Above the sewer main.
It spilled a shining waterfall out of a pipe
Somebody had gouged through the slanted earth.
Sixteen thousand and five hundred more or less people
In Martins Ferry, my home, my native country,
Quickened the river
With the speed of light.
And the light caught there
The solid speed of their lives
In the instant of that waterfall.
I know what we call it
Most of the time.
But I have my own song for it,
And sometimes, even today,
I call it beauty.

from

## This Journey

## The Turtle Overnight

I remember him last twilight in his comeliness. When it began to rain, he appeared in his accustomed place and emerged from his shell as far as he could reach—feet, legs, tail, head. He seemed to enjoy the rain, the sweet-tasting rain that blew all the way across lake water to him from the mountains, the Alto Adige. It was as near as I've ever come to seeing a turtle take a pleasant bath in his natural altogether. All the legendary faces of broken old age disappeared from my mind, the thickened muscles under the chins, the nostrils brutal with hatred, the murdering eyes. He filled my mind with a sweet-tasting mountain rain, his youthfulness, his modesty as he washed himself all alone, his religious face.

For a long time now this morning, I have been sitting at this window and watching the grass below me. A moment ago there was no one there. But now his brindle shell sighs slowly up and down in the midst of the green sunlight. A black watchdog snuffles asleep just beyond him, but I trust that neither is afraid of the other. I can see him lifting his face. It is a raising of eyebrows toward the light, an almost imperceptible turning of the chin, an ancient pleasure, an eagerness.

Along his throat there are small folds, dark yellow as pollen shaken across a field of camomilla. The lines on his face suggest only a relaxation, a delicacy in the understanding of the grass, like the careful tenderness I saw once on the face of a hobo in Ohio as he waved greeting to an empty wheat field from the flatcar of a freight train.

But now the train is gone, and the turtle has left his circle of empty grass. I look a long time where he was, and I can't find a footprint in the empty grass. So much air left, so much sunlight, and still he is gone.

## The Sumac in Ohio

Toward the end of May, the air in southern Ohio is filling with fragrances, and I am a long way from home. A great place lies open in the earth there in Martins Ferry near the river, and to this day I don't know how it came to be. Maybe the old fathers of my town, their white hair lost long since into the coal smoke and the snow, gathered in their hundreds along the hither side of the B&O railroad track, presented whatever blades and bull tongues they could spare, and tore the earth open. Or maybe the gully appeared there on its own, long before the white-haired fathers came, and the Ohio changed its direction, and the glacier went away.

But now toward the end of May, the sumac trees on the slopes of the gully are opening their brindle buds, and suddenly, right before my eyes, the tough leaf branches turn a bewildering scarlet just at the place where they join the bough. You can strip the long leaves away already, but the leaf branch is more thoroughly rooted into the tree than the trunk itself is into the ground.

Before June begins, the sap and coal smoke and soot from Wheeling Steel, wafted down the Ohio by some curious gentleness in the Appalachians, will gather all over the trunk. The skin will turn aside hatchets and knife blades. You cannot even carve a girl's name on the sumac. It is viciously determined to live and die alone, and you can go straight to hell.

# A Reply to Matthew Arnold on My Fifth Day in Fano

"In harmony with Nature? Restless fool . . . Nature and man can never be fast friends . . ."

It is idle to speak of five mere days in Fano, or five long days, or five years. As I prepare to leave, I seem to have just arrived. To carefully split yet another infinitive, I seem to have been here forever or longer, longer than the sea's lifetime and the lifetimes of all the creatures of the sea, than all the new churches among the hill pastures and all the old shells wandering about bodiless just off the clear shore. Briefly in harmony with nature before I die, I welcome the old curse:

a restless fool and a fast friend to Fano, I have brought this wild chive flower down from a hill pasture. I offer it to the Adriatic. I am not about to claim that the sea does not care. It has its own way of receiving seeds, and today the sea may as well have a flowering one, with a poppy to float above it, and the Venetian navy underneath. Goodbye to the living place, and all I ask it to do is stay alive.

# A True Voice

*for Robert Bly*

In northern Minnesota the floors of the earth are covered with white sand. Even after the sun has gone down beyond the pine trees and the moon has not yet come across the lake water, you can walk down white roads. The dark is a dark you can see beyond, into a deep place here and there. Whatever light there is left, it has room enough to move around in. The tall thick pines have all disappeared after the sun. That is why the small blue spruces look so friendly when your eyes feel at home in the dark. I never touched a blue spruce before the moon came, for fear it would say something in a false voice. You can only hear a spruce tree speak in its own silence.

## The Ice House

The house was really a cellar deep beneath the tower of the old Belmont Brewery. My father's big shoulders heaved open the door from the outside, and from within the big shoulders of the ice-man leaned and helped. The slow door gave. My brother and I walked in delighted by our fear, and laid our open palms on the wet yellow sawdust. Outside the sun blistered the paint on the corrugated roofs of the shacks by the railroad; but we stood and breathed the rising steam of that amazing winter, and carried away in our wagon the immense fifty-pound diamond, while the old man chipped us each a jagged little chunk and then walked behind us, his hands so calm they were trembling for us, trembling with exquisite care.

# The Journey

Anghiari is medieval, a sleeve sloping down
A steep hill, suddenly sweeping out
To the edge of a cliff, and dwindling.
But far up the mountain, behind the town,
We too were swept out, out by the wind,
Alone with the Tuscan grass.

Wind had been blowing across the hills
For days, and everything now was graying gold
With dust, everything we saw, even
Some small children scampering along a road,
Twittering Italian to a small caged bird.
We sat beside them to rest in some brushwood,
And I leaned down to rinse the dust from my face.

I found the spider web there, whose hinges
Reeled heavily and crazily with the dust,
Whole mounds and cemeteries of it, sagging
And scattering shadows among shells and wings.
And then she stepped into the center of air
Slender and fastidious, the golden hair
Of daylight along her shoulders, she poised there,
While ruins crumbled on every side of her.
Free of the dust, as though a moment before
She had stepped inside the earth, to bathe herself.

I gazed, close to her, till at last she stepped
Away in her own good time.

Many men
Have searched all over Tuscany and never found
What I found there, the heart of the light
Itself shelled and leaved, balancing
On filaments themselves falling. The secret
Of this journey is to let the wind
Blow its dust all over your body,
To let it go on blowing, to step lightly, lightly
All the way through your ruins, and not to lose
Any sleep over the dead, who surely
Will bury their own, don't worry.

## Butterfly Fish

Not five seconds ago, I saw him flutter so quick
And tremble with so mighty a trembling,
He was gone.
He left this clear depth of coral
Between his moments.
Now, he is here, back,
Slow and lazy.
He knows already he is so alive he can leave me alone,
Peering down, holding his empty mountains.
Happy in easy luxury, he grazes up his tall corals,
Slim as a stallion, serene on his far-off hillside,
His other world where I cannot see
His secret face.

## Yes, But

Even if it were true,
Even if I were dead and buried in Verona,
I believe I would come out and wash my face
In the chill spring.
I believe I would appear
Between noon and four, when nearly
Everybody else is asleep or making love,
And all the Germans turned down, the motorcycles
Muffled, chained, still.

Then the plump lizards along the Adige by San Giorgio
Come out and gaze,
Unpestered by temptation, across the water.
I would sit among them and join them in leaving
The golden mosquitoes alone.
Why should we sit by the Adige and destroy
Anything, even our enemies, even the prey
God caused to glitter for us
Defenseless in the sun?
We are not exhausted. We are not angry, or lonely,
Or sick at heart.
We are in love lightly, lightly. We know we are shining,
Though we cannot see one another.
The wind doesn't scatter us,
Because our very lungs have fallen and drifted
Away like leaves down the Adige,
Long ago.

We breathe light.

# Honey

My father died at the age of eighty. One of the last things he did in his life was to call his fifty-eight-year-old son-in-law "honey." One afternoon in the early 1930's, when I bloodied my head by pitching over a wall at the bottom of a hill and believed that the mere sight of my own blood was the tragic meaning of life, I heard my father offer to murder his future son-in-law. His son-in-law is my brother-in-law, whose name is Paul. These two grown men rose above me and knew that a human life is murder. They weren't fighting about Paul's love for my sister. They were fighting with each other because one strong man, a factory worker, was laid off from his work, and the other strong man, the driver of a coal truck, was laid off from his work. They were both determined to live their lives, and so they glared at each other and said they were going to live, come hell or high water. High water is not trite in southern Ohio. Nothing is trite along a river. My father died a good death. To die a good death means to live one's life. I don't say a good life.

I say a life.

## With the Gift of a Fresh New Notebook
## I Found in Florence

On the other side of the bridge,
Over the Arno,
Across the Ponte Vecchio, across
The street from the Pitti Palace, below the garden,
Under the shadow of the fortress,
I found this book,
This secret field of the city down over the hill
From Fiesole.

Nobody yet has walked across and sat down
At the edge under a pear tree
To savor the air of the natural blossoms and leave them
Alone, and leave the heavy place alone.

The pages have a light spirit
That will rise into blossom and harvest only
After your hand touches them.
Then the book will grow
Lighter and lighter as the seasons pass.
But, so far, this field is only
A secret of snow.

Now this slender field lies only a little uphill
From the river, and the pale water
Seems to be turning everything
It mirrors into snow.
It is that snow before anyone
Has walked across it
Slowly as children walk on their way to school

In the glittering Ohio morning,
Or quickly as the breathless
Ermine scamper upward through the light crust
In one indeterminate spot and then stitch
A threadwork across the whiteness and suddenly
Vanish as though blown like flakes back upward.

Red and white flowers lie quietly all around
The edges of the field,
And it doesn't matter that they don't grow there now.
For one time they grew there
Long enough to make the air
Vivid when they vanished.

I suppose I could imagine
The trees that haven't yet grown here.
But I would rather leave them to find their way
Alone, like seedlings lost in a cloud of snowflakes.
I would rather leave them alone, even
In my imagination, or, better still,
Leave them to you.

## Leaving the Temple in Nîmes

And, sure enough,
I came face to face with the spring.
Down in the wet darkness of the winter moss
Still gathering in the Temple of Diana,
I came to the trunk of a huge umbrella pine
Vivid and ancient as always,
Among the shaped stones.
I couldn't see the top of the branches,
I stood down there in the pathway so deep.
But a vine held its living leaves all the way down
To my hands. So I carry away with me
Four ivy leaves:

In gratitude to the tall pale girl
Who still walks somewhere behind the pine tree,
Slender as her hounds.
In honor of the solitary poet,
Ausonius, adorer of the southern hillsides
Who drank of the sacred spring
Before he entered this very holy place
And slowly tuned the passionate silver
Of his Latin along the waters.

And I will send one ivy leaf, green in winter,
Home to an American girl I know.
I caught a glimpse of her once in a dream,
Shaking out her dark and adventurous hair.

She revealed only a little of her face
Through the armful of pussy willow she gathered
Alive in spring,
Alive along the Schuylkill in Philadelphia.

She will carry this ivy leaf from Diana's pine
As she looks toward Camden, across the river,
Where Walt Whitman, the chaste wanderer
Among the live-oaks, the rain, railyards and battlefields,
Lifts up his lovely face
To the moon and allows it to become
A friendly ruin.
The innocent huntress will come down after dark,
Brush the train smoke aside, and leave alone together
The old man rooted in an ugly place
Pure with his lovingkindness,
And a girl with an ivy leaf revealing her face
Among fallen pussy willow.

## A Winter Daybreak Above Vence

The night's drifts
Pile up below me and behind my back,
Slide down the hill, rise again, and build
Eerie little dunes on the roof of the house.
In the valley below me,
Miles between me and the town of St. Jeannet,
The road lamps glow.
They are so cold, they might as well be dark.
Trucks and cars
Cough and drone down there between the golden
Coffins of greenhouses, the startled squawk
Of a rooster claws heavily across
A grove, and drowns.
The gumming snarl of some grouchy dog sounds,
And a man bitterly shifts his broken gears.
True night still hangs on,
Mist cluttered with a racket of its own.

Now on the mountainside,
A little way downhill among turning rocks,
A square takes form in the side of a dim wall.
I hear a bucket rattle or something, tinny,
No other stirring behind the dim face
Of the goatherd's house. I imagine
His goats are still sleeping, dreaming
Of the fresh roses
Beyond the walls of the greenhouse below them
And of lettuce leaves opening in Tunisia.

I turn, and somehow
Impossibly hovering in the air over everything,
The Mediterranean, nearer to the moon
Than this mountain is,
Shines. A voice clearly
Tells me to snap out of it. Galway
Mutters out of the house and up the stone stairs
To start the motor. The moon and the stars
Suddenly flicker out, and the whole mountain
Appears, pale as a shell.

Look, the sea has not fallen and broken
Our heads. How can I feel so warm
Here in the dead center of January? I can
Scarcely believe it, and yet I have to, this is
The only life I have. I get up from the stone.
My body mumbles something unseemly
And follows me. Now we are all sitting here strangely
On top of the sunlight.